Integrating S
Your ELA Curr........

In this helpful book, you'll learn how to seamlessly infuse social-emotional learning into your middle school English language arts curriculum. With the growing emphasis on student assessment and learning outcomes, many teachers find they lack the time and the encouragement to begin implementing SEL techniques into their instruction. This book offers a solution in the form of practical lesson plans—all of which can be implemented without tedious preparation and all of which are designed to boost self-awareness, self-management, social awareness, and other key SEL skills. Your students will discover how to . . .

- Practice mindfulness and think positively,
- Exert self-control and employ self-management skills,
- Become independent thinkers and make sound decisions,
- Be resilient and develop a growth mindset,
- Improve relationship skills and avoid bullying,
- Be authentic and develop leadership skills,
- And much more!

Each activity is ELA-focused, so students will develop social-emotional learning while meeting key literacy objectives such as reading a nonfiction speech, looking closely at symbolism, analyzing Shakespearean sonnets, and more. The book also includes reproducible tools for classroom use. You can photocopy them or download them as eResources from www.routledge.com/9781138345263.

John Dacey is Professor Emeritus of the Lynch School of Education at Boston College in Massachusetts. He is an expert on SEL and anxiety disorders and has a nationally tested COPE program used by parents, teachers, and psychotherapists to relieve the symptoms of anxiety syndrome. He is the author of 18 books on anxiety, creativity, and human development.

Lindsey Neves Baillargeron teaches English language arts to grades 6 through 12 in the North Attleboro Public School District in Massachusetts. She has integrated SEL into curricula, presented professional development workshops on emotional intelligence, and served on the SEL District Steering Committee. She has also served as a member of the Social-Emotional Learning Alliance for Massachusetts.

Nancy Tripp has taught general education and inclusion English language arts, as well as language-based classes and Tier 2 reading instruction to grades 5 through 8 for 25 years in Westport, Massachusetts. She loves curriculum work and has presented numerous professional development workshops, study groups, and summer institutes.

Also Available From Routledge Eye On Education
(www.routledge.com/eyeoneducation)

Integrating SEL into Your Curriculum:
Practical Lesson Plans for Grades 3–5
John Dacey, Gian Criscitiello, and Maureen Devlin

Passionate Learners, 2nd Edition:
How to Engage and Empower Your Students
Pernille Ripp

Passionate Readers:
The Art of Reaching and Engaging Every Child
Pernille Ripp

Learning on Your Feet:
Incorporating Physical Activity into the K–8 Classroom
Brad Johnson and Melody Jones

Motivating Struggling Learners:
10 Ways to Build Student Success
Barbara R. Blackburn

History Class Revisited:
Tools and Projects to Engage Middle School Students
in Social Studies
Jody Passanisi

The Flexible ELA Classroom:
Practical Tools for Differentiated Instruction in Grades 4–8
Amber Chandler

The Flexible SEL Classroom:
Practical Ways to Build Social-Emotional Learning in Grades 4–8
Amber Chandler

Integrating SEL Into Your ELA Curriculum

Practical Lesson Plans for Grades 6–8

John Dacey,
Lindsey Neves Baillargeron,
and Nancy Tripp

Routledge
Taylor & Francis Group

NEW YORK AND LONDON

First published 2019
by Routledge
711 Third Avenue, New York, NY 10017

and by Routledge
2 Park Square, Milton Park, Abingdon, Oxon, OX14 4RN

Routledge is an imprint of the Taylor & Francis Group, an informa business

Library of Congress Cataloging-in-Publication Data
Names: Dacey, John S., author. | Baillargeron, Lindsey (Lindsey Neves),
    author. | Tripp, Nancy, author.
Title: Integrating SEL into your ELA curriculum : practical lesson
    plans for grades 6-8 / by John Dacey, Lindsey Neves Baillargeron,
    and Nancy Tripp.
Description: New York, NY : Routledge, 2019. | Includes bibliographical
    references.
Identifiers: LCCN 2018026568 | ISBN 9781138352575 (hbk.) |
    ISBN 9781138345263 (pbk.) | ISBN 9780429434686 (ebk.) |
    ISBN 9780429785733 (web PDF) | ISBN 9780429785726 (ePub) |
    ISBN 9780429785719 (mobi/kindle)
Subjects: LCSH: Affective education. | Emotional intelligence—Study and
    teaching—Activity programs. | Social learning—Study and teaching—
    Activity programs. | Reflective teaching. | Language arts (Middle school)
Classification: LCC LB1072 .D334 2019 | DDC 370.15/34—dc23
LC record available at https://lccn.loc.gov/2018026568

ISBN: 978-1-138-35257-5 (hbk)
ISBN: 978-1-138-34526-3 (pbk)
ISBN: 978-0-429-43468-6 (ebk)

Typeset in Palatino and Myriad Pro
by Apex CoVantage, LLC

Visit the eResources: www.routledge.com/9781138345263

Contents

Part V: Responsible Decision-Making

Part VI: Achieving Teaching Goals More Effectively

eResources

The reproducibles in this book are also available on the Routledge website as free eResources.

They are indicated in the book by the eResources logo ![logo]. You can access the eResources by visiting the book product page: www.routledge.com/9781138345263. Click on the tab that says "eResources" and select the files. They will begin downloading to your computer.

Meet the Authors

Lindsey Neves Baillargeron received a B.A. in both English and Secondary Education, summa cum laude, from the University of Rhode Island in 2008, followed by an A.L.M. in Extension Studies, concentrating in English and American Literature and Language from Harvard University in 2015. She has undergone numerous trainings on student motivation, engagement, and learning outcomes, executive functioning, trauma-informed conflict resolution, and Emotional Intelligence through the Harvard School of Education's Mind, Brain, Health, and Education Initiative, the Center for Neuroscience Applications at Bridgewater State University, and the Department of Psychiatry at Massachusetts General Hospital.

For the last 10 years, she has been teaching English Language Arts to students in grades six through 12 in the North Attleborough Public School District in North Attleborough, Massachusetts. During that time, she has integrated SEL into middle and secondary-level ELA curricula, presented professional development on emotional intelligence, and served on the SEL District Steering Committee. In addition to her work in public schools, she has served as a member of the Social-Emotional Learning Alliance for Massachusetts, a nonprofit advocacy organization that promotes the implementation of SEL practices in schools and communities across Massachusetts.

In her free time, she enjoys spending time with her husband and husky, gardening, swimming, and traveling.

John Dacey received a B.A. in Social Science from Binghamton University in 1963. He then enrolled in Cornell University, where he received an M.A.T. in social science in 1964 and a Ph.D. in developmental and educational psychology in 1966.

He joined the faculty of the Lynch School of Education at Boston College that year and still teaches there as Professor in the Arts and Sciences Capstone Program. John has a small practice as a psychotherapist, licensed in Massachusetts. He is an expert on SEL and anxiety disorders and has a nationally tested COPE program used by parents, teachers, and psychotherapists to relieve the symptoms of anxiety syndrome.

He is the author of 18 books on the subjects of anxiety, creativity, and human development, including *Your Anxious Child* and *Integrating SEL Into Your Curriculum, Grades 3 to 5* and *Grades 6 to 8*. His new book, in process and written for adults with anxiety disorder, is *"Why Don't You Just Relax?"* He has received public service awards from Newton, Peabody and Roxbury, MA.

He has three adult children: Julie (novelist and author of *The Tumbling Turner Sisters*), Jennifer (full professor and chair of Public Health, Tufts University), and Kristen (award-winning photographer). His wife, Linda, recently retired as professor of mathematics education at Lesley University. He has nine wonderful grandchildren ranging in age from 14 to 25.

Nancy Tripp graduated from the Lynch School of Education at Boston College with a Bachelor of Arts degree in Elementary Education and received her Masters of Education in Reading from Lesley College. She also completed a 300-hour Program of Education in Therapy for Specific Reading Disability at the Massachusetts General Hospital Language Clinic. She taught mathematics at the middle school level for two years in Attleborough, Massachusetts. Nancy has taught general education and inclusion English language arts as well as language-based classes, and Tier 2 reading instruction to grades 5 through 8 for 25 years in Westport, Massachusetts, where she currently teaches. Nancy loves curriculum work and has presented numerous professional development workshops, study groups, and summer institutes.

Acknowledgments

Thank you to Mitch Lyons for introducing us to SEL, and to Jim Vetter for all his work for the Social-Emotional Learning Alliance for Massachusetts (SEL4MA).

We also want to express great gratitude to our wonderful editor Lauren Davis, and Project Manager Marie Roberts for all her work bringing the pages to life, and Emma Capel for her cover design.

Last but not least, we want to offer sincere appreciation to our wonderful spouses, Dr. Linda Dacey, Justin Baillargeron, and Carl Tripp.

1

Why You Will Want to Integrate SEL Into Your Curriculum

The survival of the human race depends at least as much on the cultivation of social and emotional intelligence as it does on the development of technical knowledge and skills.

—Roger Weissberg[1]

For many years, the predominant way we provided intervention and instructional support followed a straightforward formula. We used ability grouping and, during core instruction, sent the students who needed extra support to a separate classroom. . . . We now know that this model of "pull out and replace the curriculum" isn't effective for the students who need supplemental instruction and intervention. This model even impedes the growth of teachers and students who do not need extra support. . . . This approach also promotes a school culture in which students who struggle don't "belong" to special education or specialists; instead, *all students belong to all teachers*. [They need SEL as well.] Win, win, and win!

—Lee Ann Jung[2]

We could cite many other international experts who now urge including social/emotional learning (SEL) in the general curriculum, for its own sake[3] and for the many ways it facilitates academic learning. They agree: "The need for a new accountability system [worldwide] has never been greater. Standardized testing has done little to close persistent achievement gaps by race, income, and language."[4]

Furthermore:

> When 7,000 Chicago-area students sat down for a standardized test a few years ago, they got a pleasant surprise: If they did well, they'd receive rewards ranging from a trophy to $20. It worked: The students (randomly chosen to participate in a study) demonstrated, on average, 5–6 months more learning than students not promised rewards, leading the economists who conducted the study to suggest they'd solved "the urban school problem"—bribe kids and they'll test better.[5]
>
> But there may be a different takeaway. These students had *no prior knowledge* of the rewards, so they didn't prepare any differently for the exam, or learn anything more. They just took it more seriously, and miraculously, looked six months smarter. Yet this was the same type of high-stakes exam that was used to rate their schools, leaders, and teachers—which might lead us to wonder how much trust to place in standardized measures and the accountability systems built upon them.
>
> On top of that, the two key indicators that drive most college acceptance decisions—high school GPA and entrance exams—only explain 20–25 percent of the variance in student performance in college. The rest of what predicts student success remains an "X-factor," yet research points to a handful of student attributes that seem to be powerful predictors of college success, including having a can-do attitude (feeling a sense of control over one's life and pursuing goals), a studious orientation (avoiding procrastination and buying into the purpose of a college education), and being an active learner (engaging in classroom dialogue and talking about one's studies outside of class). Together, these factors account for about *45 percent* of college success.[6]

So why is that? Why is AL (academic learning of facts and skills) so dominant in the West, and also, to a lesser extent, in the East? Emphasis on the academic core is not the major problem; the rigid multiple-choice tests used universally to measure its acquisition are. For students to succeed on these tests, they must be doggedly drilled on the correct answers. No wonder so many drop out. And what teacher enters the profession out of a love for drilling students?

Another impetus for SEL is the surging number and severity of problem behaviors, especially among secondary school students.[7] They are receiving messages about social and emotional norms through multiple media, and at a faster rate than we have ever seen before. Many of these messages are negative—selfish, cynical, and often hyper-sexual. Most teachers want to remediate this trend. They genuinely want to make a contribution to the life success of their pupils, and they don't believe that AL alone does that. Many teachers resent being forced to "teach to the test."

In our preparation for this book, we have interviewed dozens of English Language Arts (ELA) teachers in the United States, Britain, and six other countries. They all agree: schools are currently too deeply invested in academic evaluation. There is now significant evidence that nether governmental tests, nor school grades, nor college readiness tests such as the SAT in the United States are good predictors of success in life. The SATs are not even predictive of college grades (and yet we still use them to sort applicants!).[8] Nevertheless, our interviewees concur that their primary responsibility is meeting academic goals. They just don't see a separate curriculum for SEL happening.

The solution most teachers *would* subscribe to is integrating social and emotional instruction into ELA teaching. They especially espouse the idea if it can be done without losing instructional time, and without tedious preparation.[9] And it can. According to a recent meta-study in *Child Development*,[10] infusing SEL has been found to improve academic scores by between 11% and 17%! Conduct problems, emotional distress, and drug use were all significantly lower for students exposed to SEL programs, and development of social and emotional skills and positive attitudes toward self, others, and school was higher.

As the new CASEL *Guide to SEL Programs* puts it,

> Social and emotional learning can serve as an organizing principle for *coordinating all of a school's academic, youth development, and prevention activities* [italics ours]. When systemic social, emotional, and academic learning becomes the overarching framework for a district or school, the result is an organization whose integrated programing activities are greater than the sum of its parts.[11]

A recent resolution by Massachusetts in the United States proclaims its legal requirement of its school systems:

> An effective English language arts and literacy curriculum promotes social and emotional learning. Curriculum and instruction that develop students' self-awareness, self-management, social awareness, responsible decision-making, and relationship skills can increase academic achievement, improve attitudes and behaviors, decrease negative behaviors, and reduce emotional distress. In ELA classrooms, for

example, students should practice recognizing aspects of themselves in the texts they encounter (self-awareness), engaging in productive struggles with challenging texts and topics (self-management), tailoring speech and writing to audiences' needs and interests (social awareness), grappling vicariously with difficult choices faced by others (responsible decision-making), and collaborating respectfully with students from backgrounds unlike their own (relationship skills).[12]

For integration of ELA and SEL in secondary schools to work, though, several criteria must be met:

- *Teachers are busy*. SEL lessons must be well organized and easy to implement. Assuming that all teachers already know the ELA part of our lesson plans, each of the SEL strategies in this book should average no more than 30 minutes of preparation time.
- SEL must not interfere with ELA learning.[13]
- The relevancy of SEL to the required ELA curriculum must be apparent to the teacher.
- The positive effect of SEL on classroom climate—an atmosphere that fosters concentration—ought to be apparent in the classroom.

We believe this book meets all these criteria, and to date, it is the only resource that does.

Format of This Book

This book has the following features:

- Each of the SEL strategies (also called activities) are closely integrated with a typical learning goal. For example, when learning to describe themselves objectively (SEL), pupils will identify principles of characterization (ELA)—see introduction to Chapter 2.
- All ancillary materials such as charts, checklists, and stories also appear on the book's website www.routledge.com/9781138345263, for ease in downloading or printing out in multiple copies.
  The website also offers several other types of helpful materials, organized by chapter in the book.
- The book has an international orientation, with a variety of cultural exemplars.

There is one area of SEL that is the source of great conflict: sex education. Certainly it can be argued that this arena has many problems that societies around the world struggle with:

> Adolescents frequently cite mass media is a primary source of information about sex. Unfortunately, accurate, healthy, and responsible messages about sex are not typical in the entertainment media. Studies of music videos show pervasive sexual objectification and degrading sexuality, especially regarding girls and women. Other studies find regular exposure to certain sexual content on TV, glamorizing early sexual relationships and teen motherhood, was found to predict earlier sexual activity and higher rates of teen pregnancy. And with a large percentage of teen boys, and many teen girls, now being exposed to online pornography, researchers are just beginning to see the effect that images of highly unrealistic sex and bodies, and often violent, degrading sex, are having on young people.
>
> —Tamara Sobel, Director, Media Literacy Now

Few educators or adolescent psychologists would disagree with this dismal picture. What is the responsibility of SEL? We find the answers to that question to be so freighted with situational differences and with values disagreements, religious and otherwise, as to make the topic beyond the scope of this book. Sorry for the "cop out," but we can only hope that you and your colleagues will do your best to attend to it.

Indeed, the teaching profession has gone through difficult times for the past several decades, to put it lightly.[14] Much of the problem has been due to a misunderstanding of the true causes of the decline in effectiveness of public education worldwide. However, schooling is, we believe, about to be freed from this misdirection of societal complaints. We are convinced that the problems in schools today are not academic in nature, but rather the direct result of the decline of SEL. There is every indication that this imbalance is about to change. We sincerely hope that this book will contribute to that reversal.

Notes

1 Weissberg, 2016.
2 Jung, 2018.
3 A good film on the need for SEL may be found at: facebook.com/bbcnews/videos/10155512752052217/

 4 Center for Collaborative Education, 2017.
 5 Levitt & others, 2012.
 6 Goodwin & Hein, 2016.
 7 E.g., WebMD, 2017.
 8 Paulos, July, 2016.
 9 Cressey & others, 2017.
10 Taylor & others, July, 2017.
11 CASEL, 2016, p. 1.
12 Mass. ESSE, 2017.
13 Payton & others, 2015.
14 E.g., Meador, May, 2017.

Part I

Self-Awareness

2

Be Authentic

The 12 traits we espouse in this book are essential to every student's success in life. If we had to pick just one, however it would be authenticity. Without it, you cannot be a person of character, of integrity. This most important virtue is about being humble. The word does not mean being debased or self-deprecating. It means "being right-sized," which means having an accurate assessment of your assets and deficits. We all have both. The humble person is aware of this. Humility plays a central role in authenticity. It is the first of two components:

- Authentic persons are objectively aware of their own strengths and weaknesses.
- They don't pretend to be someone they aren't.[1]

Authenticity allows people to be comfortable with themselves, to being trusted by their friends, and to be leaders.

There Is Teaching, and Then There's SEL Teaching

Every teacher has seen this happen: you spend hours making corrections on students' work, only to see identical mistakes on the next assignment. The result can lead to feelings of frustration and dismay. Years ago, when I became the supervising teacher for the school literary magazine, I was amazed by the writing growth I saw in my students. What made such a difference?

Students were doing real work for a real audience, and they wanted to do well. Students had a choice in the type of assignments they had. And they were truly responsible for their work. In my typical English class, if students didn't do their work, they would get a poor grade and both of us would likely feel defeated. But on the magazine staff, if they didn't do the work, someone else would have to do it. After all, no publication leaves a big blank space that says "James didn't finish his story."

I now see that the factors that led to my students' greater academic success are the same ones advocated for in *11 Principles of Effective Character Education*.[2] You do the best you can, and then get honest feedback. We tell our students all the time: "Don't just say 'I like it!' Be kind, but be honest!"

—Lindsey Neves Baillargeron[3]

Real vs. Ideal Self

Psychologist Carl Rogers offered a good insight into authenticity, and his theory underlies our strategies. He said that everyone has two images of themselves:

- Their *ideal self*, which comprises all the traits they believe they possess
- Their *real self*, which comprises all the traits they actually have.

Rogers's insight was that the greater the distance between the two, the great the inner conflict the person suffers. There is a "war" being carried out in the psyche of the conflicted person, which makes it harder for him[4] to be authentic. Such a person lacks self-knowledge, and therefore the power

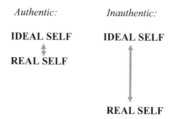

Figure 2.1 Two Ends of the Authenticity Continuum

he needs to be all he can be. He cannot be trustworthy, and others know it. Undoubtedly, you have seen the implications of this disconnect in the classroom—students who struggle when working in groups or react inappropriately to the slightest hint of criticism. Personalities, in general, fall into two ends of the authenticity continuum:

When the distance between the ideal self and the real self is great, Rogers recommended three possible remedies:

- Lower your ideal expectations to a more reasonable level.
- Raise your real efforts to a more reasonable level.
- And (usually), both.

Knowing and showing yourself accurately is essential to being authentic, a person of character. In your classroom, authenticity leads to intrinsic motivation, which then leads to greater engagement.

Are today's youth learning to become people of character? Here's what *New York Times* editorialist David Brooks wrote recently:

> When it comes to character and virtue, young people have been left on their own. Today's go-getter parents and today's educational institutions work frantically to cultivate neural synapses, to foster good study skills, to promote musical talents. We spend huge amounts of money on safety equipment and sports coaching. We sermonize about the evils of drunk driving. We expend enormous energy guiding and regulating their lives. But when it comes to character and virtue, the most mysterious area of all, suddenly the laissez-faire ethic rules: You're on your own, Jack and Jill; go figure out what is true and just for yourselves.[5]

ESSENTIAL Questions

- How do our values and beliefs shape who we are as individuals and influence our behavior?
- What is the role of a hero or "she-roe" (coined by Maya Angelou) in a culture?
- Do we truly know ourselves?
- What is changeable within us?
- How is a hero different from a celebrity? From a saint? A role model?
- If you were to leave behind your own legacy for future generations, what would you include in it and why?

ACTIVITY 2A Sonnet Sense

ELA Goal: Write arguments focused on discipline-specific content.

SEL Goal—Self-Management: Establishing ideals that can motivate greater achievement, especially when the going gets tough.

Materials Needed: Pencil and paper.[6] **Reproducible 2A1: Shakespeare's 29th Sonnet; 2A2: Translation of Shakespeare's 29th Sonnet Into Modern Terms**

Shakespeare's 29th Sonnet

1.	When in disgrace with fortune and men's eyes,
2.	I all alone beweep my outcast state,
3.	And trouble deaf heaven with my bootless cries,
4.	And look upon myself, and curse my fate,
5.	Wishing me like to one more rich in hope,
6.	Featured like him, like him with friends possessed,
7.	Desiring this man's art, and that man's scope,
8.	With what I most enjoy contented least;
9.	Yet in these thoughts myself almost despising,
10.	Haply I think on thee, and then my state,
11.	Like to the lark at break of day arising
12.	From sullen earth, sings hymns at heaven's gate;
13.	For thy sweet love remembered such wealth brings
14.	That then I scorn to change my state with kings.

2A2: Translation of Shakespeare's 29th Sonnet Into Modern Terms

1.	When I am feeling like I am a jerk,
2.	And am sorry for myself,
3.	And complaining to everybody about it,
4.	Because I am really angry about it,
5.	Wishing life had made me a lucky guy,
6.	Someone who is good-looking and has a lot of friends,
7.	Jealous of this guy's abilities, and that guy's influence,
8.	Unhappy even with my favorite things;
9.	Almost at the point of committing suicide,
10.	Suddenly I think about you, my love,
11.	You who are like a bird flying up in the morning,
12.	One that sings beautifully.
13.	Then I realize that I am very lucky,
14.	And I wouldn't trade my life for anything!

Ask your students if they can figure out the meaning of Shakespeare's 29th sonnet (**Reproducible 2A1: Shakespeare's 29th Sonnet**). Invite a volunteer to state what is Shakespeare's message or theme?

For example, for Shakespeare's line 1, *"When in disgrace with fortune and men's eyes,"* they might interpret as *"When I am feeling like I am a jerk."*

When you think most have finished, pass out **2A2: Translation of Shakespeare's 29th Sonnet Into Modern Terms**.

1. Have each group decide, for each line, whether this translation is better than the one they developed or not, and why.
2. Now that they understand the meaning of the sonnet, they should try to identify with the character about whom it is written. Ask them to think about a time when they were seriously sad about some loss.
3. Ask them to write a piece (a brief memoir, a statement from the viewpoint of a friend, an obituary) about the experience.
4. Ask them to write three paragraphs about how they managed to get out of their depressed state. Here could they write an enumerated list (almost procedure) of what they did to get out of their depressed state?
5. Most importantly, from the standpoint of authenticity, is the willingness to share the truth about oneself with others. Therefore, ask students to volunteer to read their paragraphs to the other members of their group.
6. Finally, ask them to share their thoughts on the meaning of authenticity, and how the volunteers have demonstrated.

ACTIVITY 2B What a Hero!

ELA Goal: Recount a story, including fables, folktales, and myths from diverse cultures; determine the central moral lesson.

SEL Goal—Self-Management: Establishing ideals that can motivate greater achievement, especially when the going gets tough.

Materials Needed: **Reproducible 2B1: Malala Yousafzai: "The Bravest Girl in the World."**

Malala Yousafzai: "The Bravest Girl in the World"

Malala was a 12-year-old student attending a Pakistani school when she wrote a blog for the BBC television network. She supported the rights of girls in her country to an education, even though the ruling Taliban had banned females from attending school. As Malala gained prominence for her writing, South African Bishop Desmond Tutu nominated her for the International Children's Peace Prize.

In October of 2012, a Taliban gunman boarded her school bus and shot her three times in the face. She was in critical condition for days, but improved enough to continue her recovery and rehabilitation in England. The Taliban continued with their threats to kill her and her father, but she would not cease to speak out for her young sisters throughout southern Asia. On December 16, 2014, the day of an attack on a military school in Pakistan by the Taliban that claimed 141 lives, the great majority of them children, she said she is "heartbroken over this cowardly act."

Malala's bravery and activism for women's right to education has brought support from all over the world. A UN petition, "I am Malala," was born. The petition's focus was for all children worldwide to have the right to be educated in school by December 2015. The initiative lead to the ratification of Pakistan's first "Right to Education Bill." She has been recognized with over 30 distinguished honors and awards from many countries, including being the youngest winner ever of the Nobel Peace Prize in 2014.

1. Tell your students that a hero is someone who is admired by others. They may not have met such a person, but they should know it is someone really special. This is a person they hope to become like.
2. Ask students if they can tell you the name of such a person. If they don't have a hero now, ask them to consider one: Malala Yousafzai.
3. Read or pass out **Reproducible 2B1: Malala Yousafzai: "The Bravest Girl in the World."** Here I would include reading strategy. Emphasize this DURING reading strategy. Read, markup, and annotate "The Bravest Girl in the World." Position the text on two thirds of the paper separated by a vertical line, leaving 2–3 boxes for students to write their annotations in. This box runs along the entire text. Label this blank column Annotations/My Thinking. Tell students they should read with a pencil in hand—a DURING reading strategy. Seed their thinking with a question before they begin reading, perhaps What makes this text powerful?
4. After reading: Require each of your students to write down if they strongly agree, agree, disagree, or strongly disagree the following questions about their own personality traits. Are they:

   • Courageous, in some areas?
   • In control of their lives?
   • A leader in some areas?
   • Patient?
   • Kind?

5. Now, ask students to look over their answers in small groups, and see what each one of them reveals:

   • How is Malala like or different from them?
   • Does it make any difference that she is a girl?
   • Do they know anyone like her (older or younger)?
   • What could they do to be as authentic as she clearly is?

ACTIVITY 2C Behind the Classroom Door

ELA Goal: Write informative/explanatory texts.

SEL Goal—Self-Awareness: Introduce students to thinking about the true nature of their own personality, through a projective method.

Most adolescents have only begun to be self-aware. This strategy provides them with a means of thinking about who they are without the usual influences of pride or defensiveness. The technique is called "projection": stating what you really think about yourself without being aware you're doing it.

Materials Needed: None.

Suggest to each of your students that he[7] imagine himself standing in a classroom, behind an open door. Tell him to imagine that a small group of his friends is standing out in they are hallway. You can hear them talking about you, but they're not aware that you're nearby. One of those friends says, "I really like [your name] because he's so . . . [smart? cute? kind?]"

1. Each student should write down their name and their answer to this question on paper, privately.
2. Now ask the class to suppose another member of the group in the hall says, "Well, there is one thing I think is not so great about [your name]."
3. Ask each student what he thinks that person is probably saying about him. Repeat this same sequence of these two questions two more times, so each of your pupils will have six words describing themselves, three positive and three negative. The papers should be turned in to you so you can evaluate the answers in terms of both academic and SEL goals.
4. For each of the three positive and three negative adjectives students wrote on their papers, ask them to say why they think that adjective was applied to them ["Because it's true? Because she likes me? Because he's lying?"]. Also ask which of the six adjectives really are true, and whether it hurt their feelings to "hear" the negative remarks.

   Allow us to give you this example of the sequence provided by one of the authors' ninth-grade grandson (Dacey):

   Positive trait: "Kind." Do you think they are right? "Yes." Why do you think so? "Because if another kid in class is crying, I go up and put my arm around him." What about a negative trait? "Talks too much." Do you think they are right? "Yes." Why do you think you talk too much? "Because I would rather listen to me than anyone else!"

5. Now ask each of your students to think about the following questions without having to write anything down:

- Are you willing to discuss your answers in your small group?
- Would you like everyone to know about the good things those friends out in the hall might have said about you?
- How would you feel if everyone knew the bad things they might have said about you?
- Do you think it's good for people to know everything about you, even if some of those things hurt your feelings? Why or why not?

Mention Dacey's law: "Do not worry what people are thinking about you— they aren't!"

ACTIVITY 2D My Personal Shield

ELA Goal: Generate and compare multiple possible solutions to problems; use words and drawings to symbolize personal attributes.

SEL Goal—Self-Awareness: Seek to build a better understanding of one's own personal traits.

Materials Needed: **Reproducible 2D1: Personal Family Shield, Reproducible 2D2: Personal Shield Blank.**

Personal Family Shield

Personal Shield Blank

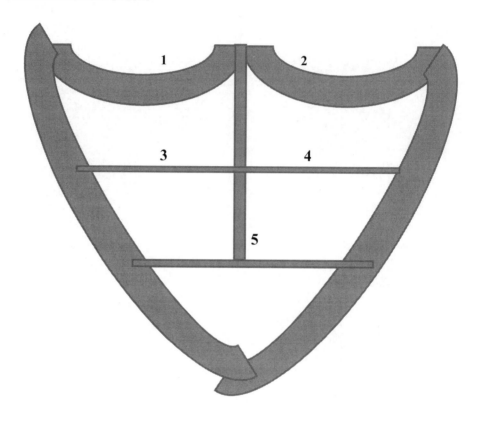

Show the class the example of a real family shield (**Reproducible 2D1: Personal Family Shield**).

Ask for guesses about why some people like to have such a shield. [In the traditions of England and Scotland, a shield or crest refers to the individual's "coat of arms." This art work appears on a shield. This individual was typically a knight of the realm, and the shield celebrated his achievements through symbols, such a lion.]

Now, pass out copies of the shield presented in **Reproducible 2D2: Personal Shield Blank**. They should draw symbols in each of the five sections of the shield that represent their answers to the following questions:

1. What is a symbol that stands for a skill you are really good at? [For example, if a student thinks he is a good tennis player, he might draw a tennis racket or a tennis ball or a tennis net.]
2. What is a symbol that stands for a skill that you are really bad at?
3. What is a symbol that stands for the personality trait that shows what a good person you are? [An example might be the trait of kindness, the symbol might be of a stick figure who is crying, and another stick figure putting her arm around him.]
4. What is a symbol that stands for the personality trait that shows that you are not such a good person?
5. What is a symbol that could stand for who you are as a whole person, that would represent the total view of you to the world? [For instance, the picture might be of the person standing on the stage with lots of stick figures in the audience applauding.]

Now form groups of four. Instruct students to show their shield, one at a time, to the other three, who try to guess what the icons on the shield stand for. When each student has related the meaning of his symbols, you might have each of them write a brief paragraph. Now Flashdraft on how this exercise made them feel.

If you feel comfortable doing so, you might ask the students in each group if what they heard seems true to them. This will allow each shield-maker to get important feedback from others about the truth of what they see in themselves. The potential for seriously hurt feelings is obvious, however, so you will have to do what you think is right about this suggestion.

You (the teacher) might want to look into whole programs designed for classrooms to enhance authenticity. Can you see how this strategy fits the overall objectives of SEL (and ELA)? Would you agree that preparation for this type of lesson is not too demanding of your time? Is it worth the trouble?

Notes

1 Sipos, 2014.
2 Character.org, 2016.
3 Lindsey Neves Baillargeron, Sixth-grade teacher in North Attleborough, Massachusetts, personnel communication.
4 In an effort to resolve the gender problem, we use the female pronoun in odd-numbered chapters and the male pronoun in even-numbered chapters.
5 Brooks, 2006.
6 From here on, we will assume the paper and pencils are available for all activities.
7 Remember, we only use the male pronoun because this is an even-numbered chapter. We mean these instructions for female students, too.

3

Practice Mindfulness

The concept of mindfulness is not new. Meditation, for instance, is ancient, but recent research has improved our grasp of its uses. The father of research on mindfulness, psychiatrist Jon Kabat-Zinn, says it is "the awareness that emerges through paying attention on purpose, in the present moment, and nonjudgmentally to the unfolding of experience."[1] Most of us, he says, miss all kinds of important information, about ourselves as well as others. We lack attentiveness.

Psychologist Ellen Langer says that the *unmindful* person is one who "*is often in error, but seldom in doubt*."[2] This is because that individual has come to believe most of the information she has is unquestionably true, and therefore she no longer needs to pay it any mind. The essence of mindfulness, however, is paying attention.

At least eight advantages to mindfulness of one's health have been documented.[3] It can:

- Enhance brain performance.
- Promote creative thinking.
- Alleviate stress.
- Curtail anxiety.
- Increase compassion.
- Decrease depression.
- Minimize chronic pain.
- Lower risk of heart attack or stroke.

ESSENTIAL Questions

- How can mindfulness improve our skills in descriptive writing?
- How can a broad vocabulary help us to be mindful?
- How can mindfulness help us in our daily lives?

ACTIVITY 3A What Are Sensory Details?

ELA Goal: Analyze how an author develops setting in a story; analyze how setting creates a particular mood in a story; develop descriptive skills in narrative writing; improve word choice.

SEL Goal—Self-Awareness: Become more mindful of sensory experiences; develop emotional vocabulary and ability to notice the present moment; build resilience.

Self-Management: Recognize the powerful effects of mindfulness; develop as a tool for self-management in times of difficulty.

Materials Needed: Pencil and paper (or journal if you use journals), **Reproducible 3A1: Sensory Detail Map Activity Sheet**.

Sensory Detail Map Activity Sheet

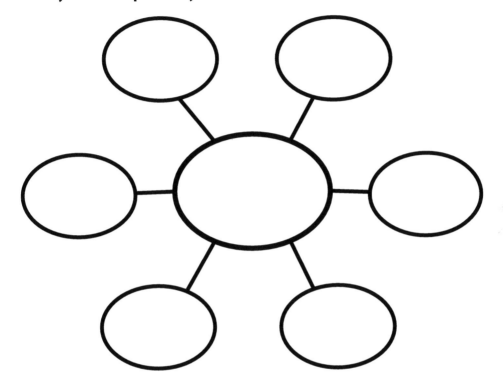

Introduction: What is mindfulness?

Suggestion: One great way to introduce complicated concepts is through the use of trade books, or children's literature. There are plenty of wonderful books out there that introduce young students to mindfulness, but two of my favorite books are *Breathe and Be: A Book of Mindfulness Poems* by Kate Coombs, and *I Am Peace: A Book of Mindfulness* by Susan Verde.

Explain how one easy way to practice mindfulness is to observe our experience through the five senses. Writers use their senses to create whole worlds for their readers. When we see a writer describing something through the five senses, the writer is using a writing technique called sensory details.

What are sensory details?

Sensory details are descriptions of sensory experiences (something we can experience with one of our senses) that an author uses to make a setting feel real to the reader. Sensory details help us to be able to picture specific places or events in our minds. If you were writing a story about this class, how would you describe the setting?

Guided Practice

1. Introduce **Reproducible 3A1: Sensory Detail Map Activity Sheet**: In the middle of the brainstorm web, write your setting "Room _____." Notice the six senses listed on the brainstorm web (see, hear, taste, feel [physical], feel [mental], smell).
2. Model one descriptive/sensory detail for each sense depending on what you experience in the room.
3. Give students 5 minutes (and stress that to do this exercise effectively, it must be very quiet so you can hear the softer sounds in the room), and have them write down as many sensory details as they notice. Strive for at least two more per sense. Tell them that you will let them know when 5 minutes is up.
4. After 5 minutes is up, have them write a paragraph describing the classroom. Optional: Provide a sentence starter: "When you walk into Room _____, you may notice . . ."

   Have students "Turn and Talk" to discuss what they experienced as a class. Emphasize how we can be in the same room, but notice different details
5. **Challenge: Take two of your sensory details from **Reproducible 3A1: Sensory Detail Map Activity Sheet** and turn them into examples of figurative language (simile, metaphor, alliteration,

personification, hyperbole). Define figurative language terms if needed.

Follow-Up Questions

1. What was it like to try to pause and tune in to what was going on around you? Was it easy? Difficult? Why?
2. What did you notice when you tried to be mindful of the present moment?
3. Are there any times when practicing mindfulness might be helpful? If so, when?

Sensory Detail Game: Day 2 of Sensory Detail Lesson

Materials Needed: Index cards with various settings (one per index card), folded up; a box, bucket, or basket to hold the different index cards; chart paper; markers; tape.

Examples of settings: the beach, forest, a sports game (you pick the sport), a movie theater, the grocery store, a theme park, a park, a restaurant.

1. Separate class into groups of three or four.
2. Each group gets a folded-up index card with a specific setting. They must keep this setting a secret from other groups in the class, as the object of the game is to describe it so well that their classmates can guess the location based on their descriptions.
3. On the chart paper, groups will draw a sensory detail brainstorm map just like the one that they were given for the first activity on **Reproducible 3A1: Sensory Detail Map Activity Sheet**, with six senses in the outer legs. For this round, they are to leave the middle circle blank, so their peers can guess the setting.
4. With their group members, students are to imagine this setting in their minds, and come up with as many sensory details as they can. Remember: the objective is to be so descriptive that their classmates should be able to guess the setting based on the sensory details. This should take 10–15 minutes.
5. Each group presents their sensory detail map and the class tries to guess the location.

Wrap-Up: Revisit essential questions; have students write their thoughts on index cards as a "Ticket to Leave" for the day. Use these as review in tomorrow's class.

ACTIVITY 3B "A Dream Deferred" and Mindful Eating

ELA Goal: Analyze how an author uses figurative language to create meaning and develop literary elements such as theme in a text.

SEL Goal—Self-Awareness: Become more mindful of sensory experiences; develop emotional vocabulary and understanding of adverse experiences; build resilience, growth mindset.

Materials Needed: Pencil and paper, **Reproducible 3B1: "A Dream Deferred" and Mindful Eating**, grapes (enough so that each students has one) and raisins, small paper plates, art reproducible, highlighters (optional). Variation: Have students work in partners where one is in charge of describing the grape and one in charge of describing the raisin.

"A Dream Deferred" and Mindful Eating

Read the poem "Harlem" by Langston Hughes, available here:
www.poetryfoundation.org/poems/46548/harlem

Annotate it line by line.

Poem Annotations

Mindful Eating

Guiding Sensory Questions	grape	raisin
Sight: Notice what colors it is. It may not just be purple or green, but a specific shade of purple or green. What shade is it? Does it have different colors on it? Specks of a lighter purple or a darker green? How does the light hit it? What is its shape? Is it perfectly round or is it more ovular?		
Touch: How would you describe its texture? Is it plump? Squishy? Soft? Is it smooth? Dry?		
Smell: What does it smell like? Is it sweet? Fresh? Maybe it smells like spring time or summertime or the air after it has rained. . . . What does it smell like to you?		
Sound and taste: Now we are going to eat it but not all at once. Do not bite and swallow it immediately or you will miss the next few steps. What does it taste like? How would you describe its flavor? Sweet? Sour? Tangy? What does it sound like when you bite into it? Does it "snap"? Does it "squish"? What word can you make up to describe its sound?		
Now imagine that this grape represents a dream or a goal you have when you first think of it; that moment when it feels fresh and you are filled with excitement. What do you think he is trying to tell you about what a dream or goal looks like, sounds like, feels like, smells like and tastes like? What is it like when it is put off over time?		

Journal Prompt Quick-Write

Describe a time when you wanted something very badly, but you were not able to get it. It could be a gift that you had hoped to receive, a chance to play on a specific sports team, or a particular role in a play. How did you feel? What did you do with this feeling?

This lesson works well as an introduction to simile and metaphor, as a guided practice activity, or as a review.

Introduce (or Review) the Definition of Each

Simile: a comparison between two unlike things using the words "like" or "as" (examples: "Her hair is as yellow as the sun" or "Their steps were as loud as thunder").

Metaphor: a comparison between two unlike things in which the writer says that one thing directly *is* something else ("My happiness is a bright sun" or "The pillow was a soft cloud").

Literal vs. Figurative:

- In each of these examples, is the writer being literal or figurative? Is the girl's hair *literally* the sun? Is the pillow *literally* a cloud?
- Why do writers use figurative language? How does it help them to get a certain idea or feeling across? Why do writers use figurative language instead of just telling you what they want you to think and feel? How might it be more interesting/entertaining/suspenseful?

   **deferred: (adj.) put off over time.

Pass out **Reproducible 3B2: Mindful Eating**.

Have the students note the figurative language that Hughes uses in this poem. Focus on the first image: the "raisin in the sun." Ask students: what is a raisin before it becomes a raisin? (A grape.) What is a dream before it is deferred or put off over time? How does his simile show this?

This mindful activity asks students to describe the grape and raisin using sensory details, and to then draw parallels between the objects and then dreams deferred.

Go through each of the five senses again, having the students write down their observations in the chart on **Reproducible 3B1: "A Dream Deferred" and Mindful Eating**.

Once you have done this exercise mindfully, eating both the grape and the raisin, ask these questions:

1. Think about how a grape becomes a raisin when it is subjected to the oppressive (keyword! Note: If your students have learned about the Harlem Renaissance, you may make this connection: think about the context of Harlem Renaissance and the ongoing struggle for equality) heat from the sun over time. It changes in shape, appearance, texture, taste, and smell. Most importantly, it grows smaller and smaller over time.

2. What feelings might Langston Hughes be trying to describe to you? What might it feel like when your dream does not come true over a long length of time?

3. Why do you think he uses similes to get his ideas across? How is this more interesting or emotional than if he were to just tell you how it feels?

4. Now, pay attention to the last line. How is it different? What word is missing? ("Like.") In the last line, he uses a metaphor instead of a simile, and it is a very powerful one. What happens to a dream at the end? (It explodes.) Think about it. Is he saying that it creates the FEELING of an explosion, as in strong anger? Or is he saying that the dream is destroyed and it doesn't exist anymore? Or both? You decide which one you connect with and explain why.

5. What is the theme of this poem? What is the message we get as the reader?

Extended Practice Activity: Write a letter to Langston Hughes offering him guidance or advice on how to cope, deal with, or handle this situation. What helpful message would you give him? Imagine that he is your friend and needs advice.

ACTIVITY 3C Understanding Nonfiction Texts

ELA Goal: Recognize and identify features of nonfiction texts (titles, section headings); identify main idea and supporting details; use Cornell notetaking two-column notes to become active readers of nonfiction; develop research skills in the content areas (science/psychology).

SEL Goal—Self-Awareness: Become more mindful of thoughts and feelings in the present moment; recognize and develop coping skills.

Self-Management: Recognize the powerful effects of mindfulness; develop as a tool for self-management in times of difficulty.

Materials Needed: Article (adapted for middle school readers), **Reproducible 3C1: What Is Mindfulness?, Reproducible 3C2: Guiding Questions on Mindfulness Article**.

What Is Mindfulness?

Introduction: What is mindful meditation?

Word splash on board: What comes to your mind when you see the word "mindfulness"?

Mindfulness: The Way to Improved Health and Happiness?

by Lindsey Neves Baillargeron

Essential Question: How can mindfulness help us in our daily lives?

Have you ever been unable to sleep because you couldn't switch off constant thoughts racing through your head?

Perhaps you've found yourself distracted by your own mind, making it difficult to focus on what you are trying to do in a certain moment, or maybe you've walked into a room and forgotten why you went in there. To many, this tendency that our minds have of jumping from one thought to another, never pausing to allow us to focus on the present moment, is known as "monkey mind." This pattern of mental "jumping around" can often lead to stress and struggle, or even physical symptoms such as headaches, stomach aches, or muscle tension—but the good news is, mindfulness may be the key to improving your well-being.

So what is mindfulness? According to the American Meditation Society, mindful meditation is "a simple and effortless process where you connect with the silence and peace within yourself. . . . It is a simple technique which allows the body to experience a profound state of rest while the mind becomes quiet and alert. Deep-rooted stresses are released in a completely natural way benefiting all aspects of health and well-being" (AMS).

While science has just begun to explore its benefits, literature from India and China has toted its perks for thousands of years. In the ancient Indian *Mahabharata*, the narrator advises readers to try to "quiet the mind" and become "like a log [who] does not think." Likewise, in an ancient Chinese text known as the *Tao Te Ching*, the writer encourages people to "Empty the mind of all thoughts" (Manocha).

With all this talk of reduced stress, improved health and well-being, you may wonder, how does one meditate exactly? One of the best aspects of mindfulness is that you can do it anywhere, at any time, and you don't have to be experienced to reap its benefits. You can begin while sitting in a chair, at a desk, or on the floor.

Sit with a straight back, resting your hands either on your knees or in your lap. Notice your breathing. Don't worry about breathing at a specific rate—just key in to your breath. Once you have started to notice your breath, try this: breathe in for four counts, pause at the top for four counts, breathe out for four counts, and pause at the bottom for four counts. Repeat this process, breathing in and out for five counts, or as many cycles as you'd like. After just a few moments of noticing your breath, you may start to feel a greater sense of calm relaxation.

But what if you try to be mindful and you find yourself continually distracted by your inner thoughts? Don't worry; the goal of mindfulness is not to do it perfectly—just practicing is enough. According to more than a dozen years of scientific research conducted in Australia, focusing on the breath can have numerous benefits, regardless of whether or not a person successfully "empt[ies] the mind."

Take, for instance, a 2011 Meditation for Work Stress Study that involved 178 full-time employees working in Australia. In this study, workers' stress, depressive feelings, and anxiety levels were recorded using scientifically validated measurements like brain scans and heart rate monitors before and after the eight-week program. At the conclusion of the study, participants showed significant reductions in these feelings, leading to a greater sense of well-being (Manocha).

These results were similar to a second study that examined the effects of mindful meditation on asthma sufferers as well. Participants showed both psychological and physical improvements, with a marked decrease in irritability of the airways. In brain scans, subjects exhibited reduced stress responses in the brain compared with subjects who did not practice "quieting the mind" (Manocha). This suggests that benefits of mindfulness are not only making people feel better, but are actually changing the brain itself!

With such robust discoveries in science, schools have begun to examine the possible benefits that mindfulness could provide for students as well. In one elementary school in Baltimore, Maryland, for example, students practice mindfulness regularly to help them regulate their emotions and achieve a sense of calm. Since implementing this change, the school has experienced a dramatic decrease in necessary visits to the principal's office, and the number of suspensions has dropped from four per year to zero (Bloom). Schools across the nation have reported similar findings, with reported reductions in stress and anxiety, and improvements in test scores.

With all this hype on the benefits of mindfulness in both the science and education community, one may consider adopting the practice of mindfulness as a way to a healthier and happier life.

Next, distribute **Reproducible 3C2: Guiding Questions on Mindfulness Article**

Name:
Class:
Date:

Guiding Questions

1. What does it mean to have "monkey mind"?
2. What could someone do to help themselves decrease the stress and anxiety that can come with "monkey mind"?
3. What are scientists currently interested in in terms of meditation?
4. What is one simile the author features to explain the effects of meditation?
5. Summarize the results of recent scientific studies related to meditation.
6. What have scientists discovered about the brain and meditation?

How could this information help *you* in times of stress or anxiety?

ACTIVITY 3D Mindful Listening and Illustrating Setting

ELA Goal: Improve vocabulary; analyze how an author uses imagery to create setting and mood in fiction.

SEL Goal—Social Awareness: Practice perspective-taking, communicating clearly, listening mindfully, and cooperating with others.

Materials Needed: Projector to display excerpts, or copies of excerpts to hand out, crayons or colored pencils, list of emotion words from previous activity in the chapter, **Reproducible 3D1: Mindful Listening and Describing Setting, Reproducible 3D2: Accountable Talk/Mindful Listening**.

Mindful Listening and Describing Setting

Nineteenth-century London in Charles Dickens' *Oliver Twist*:

> The public-houses, with gas-lights burning inside, were already open. By degrees, other shops began to be unclosed, and a few scattered people were met with. Then, came straggling groups of labourers going to their work; then, men and women with fish-baskets on their heads; donkey-carts laden with vegetables; chaise-carts filled with livestock or whole carcasses of meat; milk-women with pails; an unbroken concourse of people trudging out with various supplies to the eastern suburbs of the town. As they approached the City, the noise and traffic gradually increased; when they threaded the streets between Shoreditch and Smithfield, it had swelled into a roar of sound and bustle.

From *Anne of Green Gables* by Lucy Maud Montgomery:

> It was broad daylight when Anne awoke and sat up in bed, staring confusedly at the window through which a flood of cheery sunshine was pouring and outside of which something white and feathery waved across glimpses of blue sky.
>
> For a moment she could not remember where she was. First came a delightful thrill, as something very pleasant; then a horrible remembrance. This was Green Gables and they didn't want her because she wasn't a boy!
>
> But it was morning and, yes, it was a cherry-tree in full bloom outside of her window. With a bound she was out of bed and across the floor. She pushed up the sash—it went up stiffly and creakily, as if it hadn't been opened for a long time, which was the case; and it stuck so tight that nothing was needed to hold it up.
>
> Anne dropped on her knees and gazed out into the June morning, her eyes glistening with delight. Oh, wasn't it beautiful? Wasn't it a lovely place? Suppose she wasn't really going to stay here! She would imagine she was. There was scope for imagination here.
>
> A huge cherry-tree grew outside, so close that its boughs tapped against the house, and it was so thick-set with blossoms that hardly a leaf was to be seen. On both sides of the house was a big orchard, one of apple-trees and

one of cherry-trees, also showered over with blossoms; and their grass was all sprinkled with dandelions. In the garden below were lilac-trees purple with flowers, and their dizzily sweet fragrance drifted up to the window on the morning wind.

Below the garden a green field lush with clover sloped down to the hollow where the brook ran and where scores of white birches grew, upspringing airily out of an undergrowth suggestive of delightful possibilities in ferns and mosses and woodsy things generally. Beyond it was a hill, green, and feathery with spruce and fir; there was a gap in it where the gray gable end of the little house she had seen from the other side of the Lake of Shining Waters was visible.

Off to the left were the big barns and beyond them, away down over green, low-sloping fields, was a sparkling blue glimpse of sea.

Anne's beauty-loving eyes lingered on it all, taking everything greedily in. She had looked on so many unlovely places in her life, poor child; but this was as lovely as anything she had ever dreamed.

Accountable Talk/Mindful Listening

Explanation of Illustration	Listener Response
During the reading, I noticed . . .	I think it's interesting that . . .
While I was listening, I could imagine _____ in my mind. . . .	I noticed you paid close attention to the following images in the text:
I decided to include these specific images from the text in my illustration because . . .	I also noticed similar images because . . .
	I noticed different images because . . .
I chose to use the color(s) because . . .	Something that you said that I would like to learn more about is . . .
When I think of these colors, I think of . . .	I noticed you used the following colors:
These colors could represent the following emotions:	While I see how these colors could represent _____ emotions, I think they could also represent . . .
When I was listening to this section, I felt . . .	
Perhaps the author wants us to feel _____ about the setting . . .	

Introduction: Drawing can be a powerful mindfulness tool that can enhance reading comprehension and literary analysis. Students must be able to listen attentively and mindfully to understand a text, and to discuss it with a critical view. Use drawing as a way to help students understand the way in which authors use imagery to create a setting in a reader's mind, and secondarily, a mood. Use the excerpts from **Reproducible 3D1: Mindful Listening and Describing Setting** to provide descriptions of vivid settings students can illustrate as their drawings.

Mindful Listening and Describing Setting

After reading, students should share their pictures with a partner and discuss what stood out to them in the setting description to support their illustration. Students should complete the following sentence starters in their explanations and responses. Learning and practicing mindful, active listening is an essential skill for maintaining relationships. The "echoing" and validation in this exercise will help students learn how to communicate and listen effectively:

Guided Practice

Excerpt #1 PRE-READING Vocabulary:

straggling (v.):   straying or wandering

labourers (n.):   workers

scattered (adj.):   disorganized

concourse (n.):   a gathering or group

swelled (v.):   grew in size

bustle (n.):   energy; excitement

Begin by having the students read excerpt #1 to themselves. They should take note of the images the authors are using to create a visual in the reader's mind.

Next, read the excerpt aloud slowly, pausing occasionally, to allow the students to draw the setting on their sheet of paper. Students should make an effort to use specific colors for their pictures, as colors are symbolic of emotions within literature.

Repeat this exercise from **Reproducible 3D1: Mindful Listening and Describing Setting** for excerpt #2:

Excerpt #2 PRE-READING Vocabulary:

creakily (adv.):   harshly; making a squeaky sound

glistening (adj.):   sparkling; glowing

scope (n.):   room, space

upspringing (v.):   growing; springing up

airily (adv.):   lightly

undergrowth (n.):   small trees or bushes growing close to the ground

Next, repeat exercise listed on **Reproducible 3D2: Accountable Talk/ Mindful Listening**.

Reflection: Regroup as a class and ask students to describe and explain their illustrations and debrief on partner work:

1. What was it like to share your picture with your partner? What observations or questions did they share with you that you found interesting or helpful?

2. What was it like to use the Accountable Talk Sentence Starters during your discussion? Did it make it easier or difficult to share your ideas?
3. What was it like to listen actively to your partner? Did the sentence starters help you to focus on what your partner was saying during the discussion? Why or why not?
4. How would you rate yourself as a communicator in today's discussion? Why?
5. How would you rate yourself as a listener in today's discussion? Why?

Notes

1 Kabat-Zinn, 2013.
2 Langer, 2014.
3 Bergland, 2016.

Part II

Self-Management

4

Feel Positive

"Rachel" was attempting vainly to stuff her books, folders, and notebooks into the metal pocket under her desk. Miss Neves had told the students to create a "nice clean space" on their desktops. The instructions that she was about to give would help prepare them for the state test that would occur in four months. The date is a looming presence that all teachers feel—in the lunchroom, in the copy room, in meetings, in articles on the internet. "Hurry up! Get into these kids' heads! Make it work!"

Rachel kept shoving. Students were starting to look at her. The classroom atmosphere was becoming overwrought. Softly, Miss Neves told her to put the books on the floor. Rachel threw her hands in the air, stomped her feet, and began to sob. "I just can't! I can't make it fit!" Rachel was obviously struggling to cope with a disappointing outcome, and here Miss Neves was insisting that she create a "nice, clean space."[1]

Can you relate to this new teacher's feelings? Students are not the only ones in your classroom who experience the effects of stress, right? Resiliency in the face of stress is one of the most desirable traits in the SEL pantheon, because stressful situations are so common these days (see Chapter 7). If a child's stress level is high, or even moderate, *that child cannot think well*.

Stress and anxiety can cause mental or emotional symptoms in addition to physical ones. These can include:

- Restlessness
- Feelings of impending doom
- Panic or nervousness, especially in social settings

- Difficulty concentrating
- Irrational anger.

Obviously, you cannot control what happens in your students' lives outside the classroom. However, "many studies show that [young teens can] cope with anxiety. When asked how they deal with fear of receiving an injection from a doctor, many suggest thinking of a happy time, such as eating ice cream."[2] This known as "positive thinking." Expert Nira Datta documents that there are several relevant facts you need to know:

- Children as young as five are able to grasp the principles of positive thinking.
- Children get better at understanding positive thinking as they get older.
- When it is nurtured, positive thinking is a powerful coping tool and helps builds resilience in a child.
- Students should always acknowledge a negative situation or feeling. Then you can help them see their problem in a way that is positive and productive.

It is clear that you can infuse SEL into your lessons such that your students learn to think and feel more positively as they try to achieve your school's academic goals.[3]

The following activity is about serious sadness (depression). The ones that follow are all about anxiety. We choose this imbalance because, by and large, classroom teachers can ameliorate anxiety more easily than depression or anger. The latter two may be more life-threatening, and often require medication as well as psychotherapy.

ACTIVITY 4A Understanding O. Henry's *The Last Leaf*

ELA Goal: Interpret underlying meaning of a symbolic masterpiece

SEL Goal—Self-Awareness: Recognize the connection between thoughts, overall mental attitude, and actions.

Materials Needed: **Reproducible 4A1: *The Last Leaf*, by O. Henry** (slightly edited to fit early teen reading ability).

The Last Leaf, by O. Henry[4]

At the top of a squatty, three story brick building, Sue and Johnsy had their art studio. "Johnsy" was Sue's nickname for Joanna. In November an illness the doctors called pneumonia came to the neighborhood, and Johnsy was one of the first to catch it. She lay scarcely moving on her bed, looking through the small window at the side of the brick house next door. One morning the busy doctor examined her, then invited her friend Sue into the hallway. "She has one chance in ten," he said, as he put away his thermometer. "And that chance is for her to want to live. Your friend has made up her mind that she's not going to get well. I will do all that medicine can accomplish. However, she needs to commit to living!"

Sue went into the bedroom, and looked at Johnsy, who lay with her face toward the window. Johnsy's eyes were open wide. She was counting backward. "Twelve," she said, and a little later "eleven"; and then "ten," and "nine"; and then "eight" and "seven," almost together.

Looking out the window, Sue saw an old, old ivy vine, which climbed half way up the brick wall. The wind had blown the leaves from the vine until its branches clung, almost bare, to the crumbling bricks.

"What is it, dear? Tell me," said Sue.

Leaves. On the ivy vine. When the last one falls I must die, too. I've known that for three days. Didn't the doctor tell you?

"Oh, I never heard of such nonsense," said Sue, in a voice full of scorn. "What have old ivy leaves to do with your getting well? And you used to love that vine so, you naughty girl. Don't be a goose. Why, the doctor told me this morning that your chances for getting well real soon were ten to one! Try to take some broth now."

"There goes another," said Johnsy, keeping her eyes fixed on the window. "No, I don't want any broth. That leaves just four. I want to see the last one fall before it gets dark. Then I'll go too."

"Johnsy, dear," said Sue, bending over her, "Will you promise me to keep your eyes closed, and not look out the window? Besides, I don't want you to keep looking at those silly ivy leaves."

Johnsy, closing her eyes, said, "I want to see the last one fall. I'm tired of waiting. I'm tired of thinking. I want to turn loose my hold on everything, and go sailing down, down, just like one of those poor, tired leaves."

"Try to sleep," said Sue. "I must call Mr. Behrman up to be my model. I'll not be gone a minute. Don't try to move 'til I come back." Old Mr. Behrman was a painter who lived on the ground floor beneath them. He was past 70 and had a beard curling down from his cheeks. Behrman was a failure in art. Forty years he had painted without having any success. He had been always about to paint a masterpiece, but had never yet begun it. For several years he had painted nothing except now and then a piece for advertising. He earned a little by serving as a model to those young artists who could not pay the price of a professional model. He drank to excess, and always talked of his coming masterpiece. He was a fierce little old man, regarding himself as special guardian to protect the two young artists in the studio above.

Sue found Behrman smelling strongly of cheap booze in his dimly lighted den below. In one corner was a blank canvas on an easel that had been waiting there for twenty-five years to receive the first line of the masterpiece. She told him of Johnsy's belief that she would die when the last leaf on the ivy vine outside their building would fall.

Old Behrman, with his red eyes filled with tears, shouted his contempt for such idiotic ideas. "Vat!" he cried. "Is dere people in de world mit der foolishness to die because leafs dey drop off from a confounded vine? I haf not heard of such a ting. No, I will not pose as a model for you. Vy do you allow dot silly idea to come into her brain? Ach, dot poor lettle Miss Yohnsy."

"She is very ill and weak," said Sue, "and the fever has left her mind full of strange fancies. Very well, Mr. Behrman, if you do not care to pose for me, you needn't. But I think you are a horrid man!"

When Sue awoke the next morning she found Johnsy with dull, wide-open eyes staring at the drawn green shade. "Pull it up; I want to see," she ordered, in a whisper. Wearily Sue obeyed.

Amazingly, after the beating rain and fierce gusts of wind the wall had withstood through the long night, there yet stood out against the brick wall one ivy leaf. It was the last on the vine. Still dark green near its stem, it hung bravely from a branch some twenty feet above the ground. "It is the last one," said Johnsy. "I thought it would surely fall during the night. I heard the wind. It will fall to-day, and I shall die at the same time."

"Dear, dear!" said Sue, leaning her worn face down to the pillow, "think of me, if you won't think of yourself. What would I do?" But Johnsy did not answer.

The day wore away, and even though the twilight had fallen, they could see the lone ivy leaf clinging to its stem against the wall. And then, with the coming of the

© 2019, Taylor & Francis, *Integrating SEL Into Your ELA Curriculum*, John Dacey, Lindsey Neves Baillargeron, and Nancy Tripp

night the north wind was again blowing hard. Next morning, when it was light enough, Johnsy commanded Sue to raise the shade.

The ivy leaf was still there!

Johnsy lay for a long time looking at it. "I've been a bad girl, Sue," said Johnsy. "Something has made that last leaf stay there to show me how wicked I was. It is a sin to want to die. You may bring me a little broth now, and some milk, and-no; bring me a hand-mirror first, and then pack some pillows about me, and I will sit up and watch you cook."

An hour later she said: "Sue, someday I hope to paint the Bay of Naples."

The next day the doctor said to Sue: "She's out of danger. You've won. Nutrition and care now—that's all." And that afternoon Sue came to the bed where Johnsy lay, contentedly knitting a very blue wool shoulder scarf, put one arm around her, pillows and all. "I have something to tell you, my little friend," she said. "Mr. Behrman died of pneumonia today in the hospital. He was ill only two days. The janitor found him on the morning of the first day in his room downstairs helpless with pain. His shoes and clothing were wet through and icy cold. They couldn't imagine where he had been on such a dreadful night. And then they found a lantern, still lighted, and a ladder that had been dragged from its place, and some scattered brushes, and a palette with green and yellow colors mixed on it, and look out the window, dear, at the last ivy leaf on the wall. Didn't you wonder why it never fluttered or moved when the wind blew? Ah, darling, it's Behrman's masterpiece! He painted it there the night the last leaf fell."

Tell the class that we all experience hardship in our lives at one time or another, whether it is a test on which we didn't do as well as we expected, a sports game that we lost, or the loss of a loved one. Everyone needs to learn how to bounce back from hardship. This is called "grit" ("grit" is not accepted by some due to racist roots; see Chapter 7). Read or pass out **Reproducible 4A1** and inform them that this story has one person who just wants to quit, and two others who try to think positively.

Say: "Now that I've read *The Last Leaf* to you, I'd like you to do a Turn and Talk: Turn to a person sitting next to you and share with each other what you remember from this story." Then have the same partners complete this sentence that states the main point:

The main character, _____, wanted to _____, but _____.

Have partners share sentences, and then mention that the sick woman in the story falsely thinks that she is going to die when the last leaf falls. Ask the class to try to remember a time when they had a false thought that they believed to be true. What was that thought? What did they do about that thought? Could they find a way to think about it more positively?

Then ask students to write out their answers to these questions:

- Do you think the sick person has a mental problem, in addition to her physical illness? Is she sad or "depressed"? What do you think the word "depressed" means?
- What should you do if you feel frightened (or sad or angry)?
- What do you think it means to be a hero? Is there a hero in this story? Why or why not?
- Do you have a hero? Who is it? If you do not have a hero, should you get one?
- How do we know if someone is feeling sad or depressed? What do you think it feels like in our bodies and minds? What does the word "anxious" mean? When kids feel anxious, how can you tell? What do you think it feels like? How do anxious people act?
- What do you think we can learn from this story?
- Why do you think O. Henry wrote it?

ACTIVITY 4B Open to the Space Around You

ELA Goal: Support claim(s) with logical reasoning and relevant, accurate data.

SEL Goal—Self-Management: Control one's anxious over-reactions to environmental stressors.

Materials Needed: **Reproducible 4B1: Short Scary Story**.

Short Scary Story

A 10-year-old boy named Jimmy was sitting at the beach with his mother, father, and younger sister Anne. The family decided to go down the beach to the restaurant for lunch, but Jimmy said he wasn't hungry and would rather stay on the blanket. The others left, and after a little while, he got sick of doing that and walked away from the water toward the road. As he neared the road, a yellow limousine pulled up beside him. A man dressed in khakis and a green T-shirt got out of the car and opened the back door. Seated in the back seat was an extremely old man, his face twisted in a hideous smile. The younger man said just two words: "Get in!" Jimmy screamed and ran away as fast as he could. He didn't turn around until he got back to his blanket. The car and the two men were nowhere to be seen.

His family could see that he was upset, but they thought it was probably because they had been gone so long. "I know," said Jimmy's father. "Let's go over to the Ferris wheel and go for a ride." The first person Jimmy saw was the ticket-taker, a young man in khakis and a green T-shirt. "You're next," he said, grinning and pointing to the bucket seat. There sat the old man from the car!

Tell students that they will think the strategy you're going to teach them today must be magic! Explain that how they sit or lie can greatly affect the cortisol level in their blood.[5] Cortisol is a substance that moves through the bloodstream and is known as a "hormone." Its presence is the source of most anxiety. For example, it causes some people to worry a lot.

Then have students practice taking their pulse for 20 seconds by placing their fingers on the side of their neck and count the number of beats they feel, and writing that number down. Then read the short, scary story in **Reproducible 4B1: Short, Scary Story**. Now tell your students to take their pulse again and write it down. The number should be higher, because their cortisol level has gone up.

Finally tell them, "If you open yourself up by spreading your arms wide, uncrossing your legs and throwing your head back, like magic you will calm down. Your cortisol level will drop. Your pulse will slow down." Let's see if it works [repeat taking pulse as above]. How many of you got a lower pulse this time? If you have a tightened posture, with your legs crossed, your head forward, and your arms crossed on your chest, cortisol goes back up. Let's test that.

It doesn't matter if your mind is the victim of anxious thoughts, you can always use the opening-up method! Remember to use this technique when you start to become frightened, and you will usually be okay. And to be sure you remember it, write a one-page paper explaining how this technique works for you. Support your claim(s) with logical reasoning and relevant, accurate data.

ACTIVITY 4C Scrunch Those Muscles!

ELA Goal: Research and describe the science behind reducing lactic acid in muscles.

SEL Goal—Self-Management: Relieve anxiety caused by tense muscles. Especially recommended for boys.

Materials Needed: None.

This exercise would be an excellent interdisciplinary or co-teaching lesson with a science or health and wellness teacher who may be teaching the scientific method or self-calming techniques. Explain to the class that when we become fearful, nature has arranged for our muscles to become flooded with a substance called "lactic acid." This acid causes our muscles to be tense and ready for the "fight-or-flight" response. This is an ancient tactic built into our brains. When attacked by a sabre-toothed tiger, you had two choices: try to kill him with your spear, or run away as fast as you could.

Today we still have that response when we are frightened, but it doesn't work so well for us. For example, if you're giving a speech on the stage and you find yourself terrified, it doesn't do to scream at the audience to stop looking at you, or to run off the stage.

What we need to do when frightened is to get rid of some of that lactic acid. The only way to flush it out it is to tighten all your muscles. We do this by either stretching our muscles (ever notice cats and dogs wake up from a nap?), or we can tense our muscles as hard as we can.

Ask the students to try calming their nerves by tensing as many muscles in their entire body as they can. If they are in a public place like school, they will probably want to do this in a more private place (the restroom?), standing or sitting, as they prefer.

But let them practice this at their desks for now. They should start by clenching their fists and flexing their arm muscles. Next they should tighten their leg muscles, Finally, they clench their teeth, their neck, and their abdomen. Finally, maintaining the tension, they take in a deep breath, blow it out forcefully and then hold their breath for a count of 6 seconds (say one-Mississippi, two-Mississippi, up to six). Now tell them to completely relax. Assume the "open posture" (previous exercise). Notice how your heart has slowed down? Do you feel calmer? Do you think you could do this while sitting at your desk when something is frightening you or causing you stress?

Finally, ask them to research cortisol online and write about how and why it actually works.

ACTIVITY 4D Drawing Your Fears Away

AL Goal: Using words and art to create an emotional response in one's self.

SEL Goal—Self-Management: Learning to rely on mental imagery to calm fears and anxiety.

Materials Needed:

- Colored pencils.
- Ludwig van Beethoven—Symphony No. 6, "Pastoral," 2nd movement (to be shown on whiteboard, full screen): A good example may be found at www.youtube.com/watch?v=IoHpMYdTJDQ.
- Photo of two swans with their heads together (e.g., www.dreamstime.com/royalty-free-stock-image-two-swans-reflection-image6018286\).
- **Reproducible 4D1: Outline of Two Swans**.

Outline of Two Swans

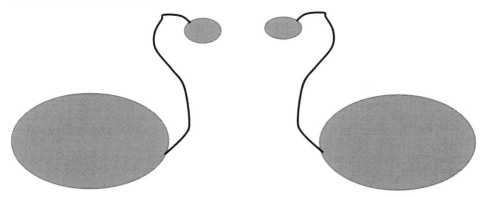

Play the Beethoven piece from his Sixth Symphony (or similar). As your students listen to it, show the picture of the two swans with their heads together.

Activate: Ask students to make a drawing of the two swans, beginning with copying the drawing seen in **Reproducible 4D1: Outline of Two Swans**. Using the colored pencils, markers, or crayons, they should elaborate on this simple line drawing until they are satisfied with their picture of the two swans. Ask them to try to associate the music they are hearing with the swans gently floating on a beautiful lake, such as the one seen in the YouTube video you are now playing. Ask students to write a paragraph on how the music and their drawing creates a specific mood. What kind of mood does it create? How could music and imagery like this example help you in times of stress or fear? Even if they are fearful: for example, a frightening task they are about to undertake, such as making a speech before the class.

Explain to them that they can keep their drawing in their desks, and whenever they feel frightened, they can take it out and try to remember the beautiful music that is now playing. Tell them that just looking at the picture will help them to calm down. Try this just before giving an exam. Give them a few minutes to stare at their drawing, trying to remember how relaxed they felt when they did it. After the test, ask them if it helped.

Stress in Your Classroom

In 1936, Hans Selye (the father of stress research) was studying the endocrine system of cows, which led to the discovery of the "general adaptation syndrome."[6] He described it as a general call to arms of the body's defensive forces. Upon further research, he found that when people (all animals, in fact) experience an initial stressor (a policeman says, "Come with me," for instance), their coping ability (e.g., blood flow to the muscles) suffers. Then, almost immediately, the individual enters a "stage of resistance." In this second stage, an almost complete reversal of the alarm reaction occurs. During this stage, he appears to have adapted successfully to the stressor.

If the stressor continues, however, eventually this leads to a "stage of exhaustion." Then the physiological responses revert to their condition during the stage of alarm. The ability to handle the stress decreases, the level of resistance is lost, and the organism weakens and eventually dies. Here is a diagram of the general adaptation syndrome. From time to time, many of your students fall somewhere on this stress continuum. Do you know which ones?

2. *Resistance* - heightened ability

+++Normal body function

1. *Shock*

3. *Exhaustion* - lowered ability - Death?

ACTIVITY 4E Describing Body Functions

ELA Goal: Compare and contrast the information gained from experiments, in particular, biofeedback.

SEL Goal—Social Awareness: Understand the effects of social stimuli on body functions. Biofeedback is a tool that provides data, often electronic, about the human body. The most common indicator is a person's heart rate or pulse, which elevates when the person is under stress. The purpose of biofeedback is to learn how to identify and control thoughts, physical sensations and behavior. For example, hearing someone shout can be scary to many children. This emotion can quickly turn to a belief that something is seriously wrong, even when nothing is. In this thought pattern, the mind/body connection will likely produce poor concentration and an uncomfortable feeling of tension and foreboding.

Materials Needed: Pulse oximeter (on Amazon for $17), **Reproducible 4E1: Tracking Sheet for the Effects of the Situation on Your Pulse Rate**.

The exercise would work well as an interdisciplinary or co-teaching lesson with a science teacher.

Tracking Sheet for the Effects of the Situation on Your Pulse Rate

Time of Day	Situation	Starting Pulse Rate	Ending Pulse Rate	Change
Ex.: 8am	*First period of class 12/11/18*	*80*	*67*	*−13*

Of course you could just take a child's pulse using your fingers and the second hand of your watch. However, the power of this instrument comes from a student watching his pulse rate number come down on the oximeter's screen as he uses various calming methods. The oximeter is a simple, portable tool that clips comfortably on a child's fingertip and measures heart rate, showing changes in real time. This instrument is also available at your local pharmacy or medical supply store for a higher price. Other types of biofeedback machines offer a complex of biological feedback, but they cost much more.

Pick a student and tell him that you are going to clip this device onto his pointer finger. Tell him to think of a scene from a scary movie. Now ask him to look at his heart rate number on this little monitor, called an "oximeter." Tell him write his pulse rate down on this chart **(Reproducible 4E1: Tracking Sheet for the Effects of the Situation on Your Pulse Rate)**. Now he should to try to control his feelings simply by changing his thoughts. That will make the number in the window on the monitor go down. He should relax and breathe slowly. Don't tell him anything except that his job is to notice his breathing and to think about relaxing. That will lower his heart rate.

After a few moments, have your student open his eyes and read the pulse rate on the oximeter. Almost certainly, it will be a lower number than before. Tell him to record the new number on the tracking sheet. Write down the difference between the two numbers on the sheet and talk about how he feels, physically and emotionally, with a higher versus a lower heart rate. Try this technique again, to see if he can get an even lower number. All of your students can create a tracking record over days or weeks [how long is up to you].

Practicing during a relaxed time for a period of a few weeks will help your students learn the effects of biofeedback, and understand its value during stressful times. The next step, when your students are better at lowering their pulse, is to try this exercise when they are under serious pressure, such as the day of a big test or some on-stage performance in school.

Now have students turn this experience into a writing assignment. Ask them to write a brief paper on how they think they are being effective in lowering their stress level, and why they think this works.

Notes

1 Lindsey Neves Baillargeron (co-author of this book), personal experience.
2 Datta, 2016, p. 1.
3 CASEL, 2017.
4 Henry, 1909, edited for this age group.
5 Henning & others, 2014.
6 Selye, 1976.

5

Control Yourself

Self-control is getting yourself to do (or not do) what you want to do (or not do), when that is difficult. We add the last phrase because you don't need self-control to get yourself to eat ice cream (assuming you like it). And you don't need self-regulation to get yourself to avoid turnips (assuming you don't like them).

Students who are good at self-management learn better than their peers. For example, they:

- Seek out advice[1] and information.[2]
- Commonly seat themselves toward the front of the classroom.[3]
- Seek out additional resources.[4]
- Voluntarily offer answers to questions.[5]
- Manipulate their learning environments to meet their needs.[6]
- Last but not least, perform better on academic tests and measures of student performance and achievement.[7]

These advantages make teaching self-control one of the highest priorities of SEL.

One stereotype holds that gifted people such as Albert Einstein lack self-control. Our research[8] and that of others[9] has found this to be false: most highly talented people are superior in their ability to control their emotions and behavior.[10]

ESSENTIAL Questions

- Why is awareness and management of your emotions important?
- What is a successful learner?
- How do "intrinsic and extrinsic" factors affect decisions?
- Why do people behave as they do?
- Why is it important to consider the effects of your decisions on others?

ACTIVITY 5A Learning Self-Control

ELA Goal: Use precise language and domain-specific vocabulary to inform about or explain the topic.

SEL Goal—Relationship Skills: Identify and describe five essential steps for achieving better self-control.

Materials Needed: Paper and pencil, **Reproducible 5A1: Five Doable S-C Techniques**.

Five Doable S-C Techniques

1. **Temptation**. What are your true motive(s) for undesirable behavior? What's the real reason you are tempted? Who else is involved?

2. **Replacement**. What's an alternative reward? Can you get a buddy to help? How?

3. **Gradualism**. Control sudden urges by eliminating them gradually. See, for example, **Activity 5B: Two Years to Completely Ethical Eating**.

4. **Punishment**. When you fail to be in control, you must pay the (preplanned) price. Only a friend can decide if you have failed, and deserve a penalty, and should most often administer the penalty.

5. **Self-Care**. Learn to take better care of yourself. Be your own best friend. You will be stronger if you don't see yourself as suffering. You might form a group of friends who help each other with self-care goals and methods for achieving them.

Describe a time when you did something that you knew - at the time - you should not have done. Why do you think you did this? If you could go back, would you have asked a friend for advice before acting? How might this have helped you? Ask your students if they think they are the same person as their mind. Most will agree that they are their mind. Then ask them if their own mind has ever misled them. Has their mind ever lied to them? If so (and you should get some examples of when it has), explain to them that this proves they are not the same thing is their mind. In fact, they can be in charge of their mind and this is the essence of self-management.

Repeat for your students the definition both self-control we gave at the beginning of this chapter. Ask for suggestions about situations in which self-control is called for. Then tell them there are five things they need to consider in order to improve their self-control. Pass out copies of **Reproducible 5A1: Five Doable S-C Techniques**. Ask them to answer the questions presented there. Now have them meet in their small groups and take turns reading their answers and discussing them.

Positive and Negative Asserting vs. Yielding

Actually, there are four types of self-control. Shapiro[11] has developed a model of self-control that compares four possible actions: positive and negative asserting and yielding.

Shapiro's Model of Self-Control

	Asserting	Yielding
Positive	Active control = positive asserting (dieting)	Passive control = positive yielding (undergoing needed surgery)
Negative	Over-control = negative asserting (anorexia)	Too little control = negative yielding (frightened to have needed surgery)

Let's consider an activity which demonstrates some differences between these four types of self-control.

ACTIVITY 5C Letting Her Be in Charge

ELA Goal: Students will practice speaking and listening, as well as collaborating in a group setting.

SEL Goal—Relationship Skills: Successfully give over control of the decision-making process to someone else.

Materials Needed: Paper and pencil, **Reproducible 5C1: Crossing the Poisonous Peanut Butter Pit**.

This exercise would work as a team-building activity at the beginning or end of the school year, or as a fun activity before a school vacation.

Crossing the Poisonous Peanut Butter Pit

Your job is to cross over the Poisonous Peanut Butter Pit, which is 6 feet in diameter (see Figure 5.1). It is so large that you cannot jump over it. To help you, you are given two 5-foot boards (that may not be attached to each other by nails or screws, for example). First group to solve the problem is the winner. Step one is to choose a leader for your group. That leader will whisper instructions to the group, which must be followed. If anyone has an idea about what to do, they must keep that motion to themselves. Be sure to "follow the leader."

Figure 5.1

Start by gathering your students into groups of four, with at least one female in each group. Appoint one of the girls in each group to be the leader. The goal is to experience yielding leadership to another, especially for those boys who think they should be leader. To work well, the group members must yield control to their leader. All must follow directions even when they disagree with the leader's directive. Now pass out **Reproducible 5C1: Crossing the Poisonous Peanut Butter Pit**.

"If anyone already knows the solution, ask them to please say nothing. Ready, get set, go." After several groups find the right answer, stop work and tell the class to look at the board as you draw the solution:

When the task is complete, have students write down their answers to the following questions. When they're finished, ask them to open a discussion about how it felt to follow the leader's directions:

- Did your leader do a good job? How or how not?
- Did anyone think they could do better job than their leader?
- Was it frustrating to follow directions even when you didn't want to?
- How did having a female leader make you feel?
- What are some situations in which yielding control is necessary (examples: being hypnotized, flying on a commercial plane)?

If you like, let them try to make up a new task. Outward Bound offers many exercises for intermediate pupils. Look them up online: www.outwardbound.org/.

ACTIVITY 5D Control: What Works for You?

ELA Goal: Determine the meaning and appropriateness of phrases as they are used to describe the student.

SEL Goal—Self-Management: Gain a better understanding of one's own level of self-control.

Materials Needed: Paper and pencil, **Reproducible 5D: Making Tough Choices**.

Making Tough Choices

Suppose you are walking along road on a warm summer day and your stomach is growling. You are SO THIRSTY and HUNGRY! However, you realize that the nearest place you can get food is almost two miles in either direction. Even if you run, you know that it's going to be a long time before you can satisfy your powerful needs. You can be miserable until you get to some food and drink, or you can use your mind. What should you do?

Pass out and ask students to read **Reproducible 5D1: Making Tough Choices**.

Assign them to groups of four and ask them to think of solutions to the problem presented to them. After an appropriate period of time, ask them to write down the answers to their following questions:

1. What does the term "self-control" really mean?
2. What are some techniques you might use to distract yourself from powerful obsessions?
3. How could "mindfulness" (Chapter 3) be helpful to you?
4. How could "creativity" (look it up) helpful to you?
5. Who among your friends might you want to ask what they would do in these circumstances? What is there about them that you think would make them helpful to you?
6. When you are finished with this activity, perhaps you should make a list of the techniques you find useful, and memorize it.

ACTIVITY 5E Step by Step

ELA Goal: Imagining what it means to be brave in the face of what feels like a threatening situation.

SEL Goal—Self-Management: Doing a self-improvement project when that is hard to do.

Materials Needed: Paper and pencil; five 2-foot pieces of hose or tubing; a toy rubber snake; a real snake in a glass cage, perhaps at the local zoo (the last three could be done with photos if necessary); **Reproducible 5E1: Safe "Snakes"; Reproducible 5E2: Toy Snake; Reproducible 5E3: Our Friend, the Snake**.

Safe "Snakes"

A piece of rubber hose

Toy Snake

Our Friend, the Snake

In this method for dealing with snake phobia, we recommend going through a series of steps to achieve a reduction in anxious feelings.

1. Ask your students to think about a snake.

2. Ask them to look at a picture of a snake.

    Now ask the students to think about the snake while viewing the video at this URL: www.youtube.com/watch?v=ClwIj3x24Q4.

3. Request that they handle a piece of hose while viewing this video again (or **Reproducible 5E1: Safe Snakes**).

4. Then have them handle a rubber snake while thinking about a real one (or **Reproducible 5E2: Toy Snake**).

5. Ultimately, your students may be able to touch and handle a real snake.

Now ask them to think of the situation which is personally either frightening to them, such as being bitten by a dog, or difficult for them, such as stopping biting their nails. When they have identified such a problem (they need not reveal it to their classmates), have them think of a step-by-step strategy for eliminating the problem.

In considering their tactics, they should attempt to answer the following questions:

1. The first question they must address is: how big should the steps be? They should be big enough to make serious progress, but not so big as to be extremely difficult.
2. Should there be a reward for each step accomplished, or only when the final goal is reached?
3. If there is to be a reward (or rewards), how powerful should they be? Expert B. F. Skinner recommended that a reward is only acceptable if it motivates desired behavior 95% of the time. That's a pretty powerful reward, or as he called it, a "reinforcement"!

They will be tempted to give themselves the reward even if they haven't truly achieved the target behavior. It may be better if the reward is given to them by an objective friend.

Pretty much everyone has more than one thing they don't like about themselves. If they are successful with this procedure, they might like to proceed to another phobia or unwanted characteristic, and design another step-by-step procedure to remedy that situation.

As we hope you can see, an important element in self-control is an estimation of the amount of risk a person should take. Unfortunately, we teachers often discourage sensible risk-taking, in part by encouraging the quest for the correct answers at all costs. We may even cause our students to be risk-averse.[12] A good analogy here is contact with germs. Many parents do all in their power to insure their children's cleanliness. However, children who live in sterile environments are *more* vulnerable to infection because they do not build up good immunity to infection. Kids *need* to get dirty sometimes.

And we adults need to let them take reasonable risks in other areas of their lives. How do they learn to do this? *Practice.* Only through trying to keep themselves under control as they investigate how risky things can be, and also how risk can be judged accurately.

What determines a child's risk-taking capacity? To a certain degree, genes. Some children seem to clamor for scary experiences such as riding on a roller coaster. They explore and expand, and when trouble occurs, they may be dazed but rarely daunted. Other kids are more cautious by nature. Hesitant to venture into unfamiliar territory, they want to preview the script before taking the part. This is why it is so important to support students through inevitable periods of failure or rejection. Without such periods, they cannot learn to manage their emotions or social interactions.

Withdrawing Support

The goal of all education is to make it unnecessary for us always to be present. That is, we want self-management to become engrained in everyday behavior. Thus we need to think about how and when to fade the support our students need in order to achieve mastery. You will need to be on the lookout for signs that class members have internalized self-regulation. Unfortunately, we cannot be specific in our advice on how to do this, because there is so much variation in a child's capacity for it. Age, gender, self-confidence, creativity, sensitivity, intelligence, and maturity are all factors that must be considered. What we can say is that you need to be on the lookout for opportunities to *offer practice, to model the skills, and to reward self-mastery.* Teachers who understand that these are among their most vital goals almost always do a fine job of it.

Notes

1 Clarebout & others, 2010.
2 de Bruin & others, 2011.
3 Labuhn, Zimmerman, & Hasselhorn, 2010.
4 Clarebout & others, 2010.
5 Elstad & Turmo, 2010.
6 Kolovelonis, Goudas, & Dermitzaki, 2011.
7 Schunk & Zimmerman, 2007; Zimmerman, 2008.
8 Dacey & Lennon, 1998; Dacey & Conklin, 2013.
9 E.g., Selman, 2003; Torrance, 2000.
10 Dacey & Packer, 1992; Dacey & Lennon, 1998.
11 Shapiro, 1993.
12 Sternberg & Lubart, 1995.

6

Think Independently

The ability to think independently means not being overly influenced by others' opinions. An example would be standing up for a classmate who is taunted for his choice of clothing or after-school activity. Through taking moderate risks, most adults learn to analyze situations, calculate an appropriate response, and follow their own paths. With practice, students can be taught to trust their own judgments, too.

It is important to recognize the influences that impact your students' judgments. As they develop self-knowledge and become more comfortable taking moderate risks and trusting their own ideas, they will be better able to evaluate the world around them with integrity. This does not mean paying *no* attention to the judgments of others. Rather, it means learning to become observant and objective about those judgments.

If a student's thinking becomes observant and objective, then he has a better chance of making sound decisions. Many factors contribute to our thinking, and much of the time, we are simply operating on automatic pilot. How well we think and act on the spur of the moment is a lot more susceptible to outside influences than we realize.

Some of these outside influences have a strong impact on our judgments, whether it is how much we like the color of someone's tie, or what box we check off on a standardized test next to a prompt for "race/ethnicity." Researchers have noted this "mental contamination" as often harmless (i.e., marketing campaigns), but sometimes damaging (i.e., lower self-esteem). A goal for promoting healthy SEL is to encourage students to know themselves, think independently, *and* appreciate the multiple perspectives that help inform their thinking.

The ability to think is the same as intelligence. For example, psychologist Edward deBono states that "Highly intelligent people are not always good thinkers. . . . Intelligence is just a potential. Thinking is the skill with which we use that potential." Most formal instruction in thinking occurs in school. Many educational theorists define independent thinking as a quality of utmost importance if we want to nurture a society that is creative, constructive, and collaborative. In part, the purpose of education is to help people think for themselves. The activities in this chapter will help students to learn to access their intellectual potential and develop the ability to successfully think for themselves.

ACTIVITY 6A Beginning the School Year With Curiosity: A Critical Ingredient

ELA Goal—Literacy: Interpret and explain information presented visually, orally, or quantitatively in charts, graphs, diagrams, time lines, titles, animations, or interactive elements on the Web.

SEL Goal—Self-Management: To encourage students to take an active interest in their learning to develop independent thinking and their own ideas.

Materials Needed: Newspapers and/or magazines such as *Time, National Geographic, Smithsonian, Scholastic News,* or other print/internet materials that feature current events from a global perspective; scissors; tape or glue; pencil/ pen; paper (see website links for related student newspapers and links).

1. Explain to students that this assignment will help them to introduce themselves to you and their classmates this year. Independent thinkers are curious, and they often use newspapers, magazines, and the internet to conduct research and learn about the world around them.
2. Further tell students that study driven by their own curiosity also helps them to manage their time and choices in order to engage in activities that are most interesting to them, and this assignment will also help you to prepare lessons that fit their interests as well.
3. Use the Think Aloud approach to model how you survey information and identify media images, diagrams, graphs, and stories that interest you and show the class more about you.
4. As you model your approach, include statements that reference the experiences, interests, passions, questions, future plans, and dreams that prompted you to notice the selected media. This is a great way for students to get to know you as well!

5. Pass out age-appropriate newspapers and magazines or provide a list of internet news links (see internet news links on website). Encourage students to survey the information, choose up to 10 articles or images that interest them, and create a collage of those articles and images.

6. Ask students to reflect on their collages with the following questions (could write on board or post with a projector):

   • What are the main topics of the articles and images you chose?
   • How do these topics relate to your interests, passions, experiences, and questions?
   • Do you want to read or study more about any of the topics depicted on your collage? If so, why do you want to study and learn more about those topics and how might you do that in the coming months? Note: this assignment lends itself to Sustained Silent Reading programs, in addition to explanatory and persuasive writing projects.
   • How does an activity like this help you to think about your choices, time, and behavior? How might these areas grow into greater interests and opportunities for study later?

Independent thinkers are curious and want to learn about the world around them. They use that knowledge to evaluate themselves and their choices, dreams, and direction. Independent learners establish regular patterns of reading and research to persistently develop their independent thinking, self-management, and resulting activity. Explain that they will build upon these skills throughout their study this year.

ACTIVITY 6B "The Road Not Taken"

ELA Goal: Students will analyze what the text says both explicitly and implicitly, drawing inferences from the poem.

SEL Goal—Responsible Decision-Making: Students will consider and build upon their abilities related to identifying choices, analyzing situations, evaluating solutions, and reflecting on one's choices.

Relationship Management: Students will practice communication, social engagement and teamwork in analyzing the poem.

Materials Needed: **Reproducible 6B1: "The Road Not Taken," Reproducible 6B2: "The Road Not Taken" Jigsaw Questions.**

"The Road Not Taken"

Read "The Road Not Taken," available here: www.poetryfoundation.org/poems/44272/the-road-not-taken

Annotate it line by line using the following chart.

Poetry Annotations

"The Road Not Taken" Jigsaw Questions

Questions for Stanza 1:

1. Circle the key words and phrases in this stanza. Why are these words the most important words to you? Explain.
2. What is the setting of this poem? In what season does this poem take place? How do you know?
3. What colors, thoughts, feelings, moods, or messages come to your mind when you think about this season?
4. What color do you notice in this stanza? What thoughts, feelings, moods, or messages come to your mind when you think about this color?
5. What do you think the phrase "Two roads diverged" symbolizes? How could it represent a moment a person could experience in his or her life?
6. What do you think Frost means when he writes that the path "bent in the undergrowth"? What do you picture in your mind? What does this image suggest about his ability to see into his immediate future?

Journal Prompt Quick-Write:

Describe a time when you made a decision that was difficult to make.

- What was it? Why did you make this decision?
- What was the outcome?
- If you had a chance to do it again, would you make the same decision? Why or why not?

Hand out **Reproducible 6B1: "The Road Not Taken"**

Stanza 2:

1. Circle the key words and phrases in this stanza. Why are these words the most important words to you? Explain.
2. When the speaker looks at the two roads, he notices that they both are "just as fair" and that they have been "worn . . . really about the same." Notice the word choice here. Is it easy for the speaker to decide which path to choose? Why or why not?
3. What might the speaker be experiencing in this moment? How do you know?
4. Can the speaker tell which path is "better"? Why or why not?
5. What could this imagery symbolize in one's life?
6. Give an example of personification from this stanza. What does it mean?

Stanza 3:

1. Circle the key words and phrases in this stanza. Why are these words the most important words to you? Explain.
2. What does the speaker mean when he says that "both [paths] that morning equally lay/In leaves no step had trodden black"?
3. In this stanza, the speaker says he "kept the first for another day!/Yet know how way leads on to way,/I doubted if I should ever come back." What do you think he means by this?
4. How does "[one] way lead on to [another] way" in life?
5. Why does he "doubt" if he "should ever come back"?

Stanza 4:

1. Circle the key words and phrases in this stanza. Why are these words the most important words to you? Explain.
2. How would you describe the mood in this stanza? (Note: There can be several answers to this question!) Why? What words or phrases give you this impression?
3. What comes to your mind when you imagine the speaker's "sigh"? What emotions do you hear in your mind when you think about his "sigh"?
4. What does the poet mean when he says "somewhere ages and ages hence"?
5. Although the speaker describes the paths as very similar in appearance, he ultimately makes the decision to take the "one less traveled by." What do you think he means by this?
6. Read the last line of the poem and notice how we don't know what kind of difference this "road" has made in his life. Apply your own interpretation to this poem. Do you imagine this "difference" as one that the speaker is happy about, or one that he regrets? Why?

PRE-READING Vocabulary

Text Feature:

stanza (n.):	a section of four or more lines in poetry; similar to paragraphs in prose
diverged (adj.):	separated; split apart
undergrowth (n.):	low-lying bushes or small trees
trodden (v.):	walked upon
fair (adj.):	reasonable; good
claim (n.):	choice; demand
hence (adv.):	from this time; from now

Arrange students into groups of four. Give each student in the group a different stanza to analyze with the guided reading questions. You may have them work on these alone or with a second round of groups in which they meet with other students who have been assigned the same stanza. Once they have become "experts" on their assigned stanza, they will report back to the original group and teach their peers about their assigned stanza.

Distribute **Reproducible 6B1: "The Road Not Taken"** and **Reproducible 6B2: "The Road Not Taken" Jigsaw Questions**.

Extended Practice: Imagine a difficult decision that you've had to make that has presented two choices to you. Using your **Reproducible 6B1: "The Road Not Taken"** as an example, write your own version of "The Road Not Taken," describing your thoughts as you consider both options that lead to your ultimate decision. Try to adapt Frost's voice in your poem, then share it with the class.

ACTIVITY 6C "The Man in the Arena"

ELA Goal: Students will work in groups to determine the impact of Roosevelt's use of diction and imagery, as well as his central message and purpose in the speech.

SEL Goal—Responsible Decision-Making: Students will examine and discuss the importance of risk-taking and independent thinking in one's pursuit of a goal.

Relationship Management: Students will practice communication, social engagement and teamwork in analyzing the poem.

Materials Needed: Journals, **Reproducible 6C1: "The Man in the Arena,"** chart paper, markers, **Reproducible 6C2: "The Man in the Arena" Jigsaw Questions**.

"The Man in the Arena"

"The Man in the Arena"

By Theodore Roosevelt

It is not the critic who counts; not the man who points out how the strong man stumbles, or where the doer of deeds could have done them better. The credit belongs to the man who is actually in the arena, whose face is marred by dust and sweat and blood; who strives valiantly; who errs, who comes short again and again, because there is no effort without error and shortcoming; but who does actually strive to do the deeds; who knows great enthusiasms, the great devotions; who spends himself in a worthy cause; who at the best knows in the end the triumph of high achievement, and who at the worst, if he fails, at least fails while daring greatly, so that his place shall never be with those cold and timid souls who neither know victory nor defeat.

"The Man in the Arena" Jigsaw Questions

Group 1: Choose 10 strong words or phrases from this selection that stand out to you and help you understand the meaning of the text. Write these 10 key words and phrases on your chart, and explain why they are important and/or how they help the reader understand the message of the speech.

Group 2: What do you think is the message of this speech? What can we take away from reading this selection? What evidence in the text supports this message?

Group 3: What do you think is his purpose in delivering this speech? What did he want to teach his audience? Why? What evidence supports your interpretation of his purpose?

Group 4: What type of person is he describing when he refers to "The Man in the Arena"? What character traits (adjectives) would you use to describe this type of person? What evidence from the text supports your answer?

Group 5: Theodore Roosevelt uses strong imagery to communicate his message to the audience. What are the strong images that stand out to you? Why do you think he uses such images to communicate his message? What do these images make you think and feel?

Group 6: Let's make a real world connection. Think about people you know— they could be famous or not famous—who have "dared greatly" and taken risks even though they might have faced criticism and judgment from others. Who are some examples of men or women "in the arena"? What descriptions in the text do they fit? Why? Give reasons to support your answer.

Journal Prompt Quick-Write

- On a scale of 1 to 5, with 1 being "not important" and 5 being "extremely important," how important is it to be able to think for yourself versus follow what everyone else is thinking? Explain why you chose this number.
- Now, using this same scale, when learning, how important is it to take a risk, or take a chance, even though you may not get something right the first time? Explain why you chose this number.
- In today's reading selection, we are going to examine an excerpt from a speech in which the 26th president of the United States, Theodore Roosevelt, proposes the importance of "daring greatly" despite how others may judge you.
- In preparation for our reading, describe a time in which you took a chance and "dared greatly." Perhaps you tried to play a new sport or an instrument, or perhaps you tried to make a new friend.

PRE-READING Vocabulary

critic (n.): a person who judges or criticizes

marred (adj.): damaged or stained

valiantly (adv.): bravely

errs (v.): to make a mistake

shortcoming (n.): a failure

enthusiasms (n.): extreme interest or devotion

timid (adj.): shy or nervous

Jigsaw Directions

Step 1: Separate class into six different groups.

Step 2: Each group receives a question on the text. They must work together to provide a response as well as evidence (at least two examples) from the text to support their response.

Step 3: They will present their information to the class using chart paper.

Step 4: During the brief, informal presentations, students will take notes on their reproducible.

Distribute **Reproducible 6C1: "The Man in the Arena,"** chart paper, markers, **Reproducible 6C2: "The Man in the Arena" Jigsaw Questions**.

ACTIVITY 6D "Yes or No?"

ELA Goal: Students will engage in a collaborative discussion with peers on a range of persuasive topics and issues, building on others' ideas and expressing their own clearly.

SEL Goal—Responsible Decision-Making: Students will identify problems, analyze situations, evaluate solutions, and discuss ethical responsibility.

Materials Needed: Index cards (one for each student), PowerPoint, projector or smart board, electrical tape or tape that you can use on the floor, an object to use for drawing from a lottery, **Reproducible 6D1: "Yes or No?" Reflection Questions**.

"Yes or No?" Reflection Questions

1. What were some interesting or surprising viewpoints that you heard today?
2. After hearing other students speak, did any of your views change today? If so, which ones? Why?
3. How easy or difficult was it to communicate your views? Why?
4. How easy or difficult was it to try to change others' opinions? Why?
5. Were there any times in which you felt strong emotions such as frustration, disappointment, or anger? Why?
6. How did you manage any strong emotions that arose during today's activity?
7. How easy or difficult was it to listen to others' opinions, especially ones with which you disagreed? Why?
8. How easy or difficult was it to communicate in a respectful way? Why?
9. What did you learn from today's activity?

1. Before the start of class, use a long piece of colored tape to divide the room into two sides.
2. Pass out index cards. Ask students to write a question that would spark a debate in the class about an issue that they care about. Some examples:

   - Should sports be coed?
   - Should schools sell fast food?
   - Should students wear school uniforms?
   - Should there be harsher punishments for bullying?
   - Should there be less homework?
   - Should middle school students still have a bedtime?
   - Should the school lunch menu have more choices?
   - Should school sports be mandatory?
   - Do kids watch too much television?
   - Should kids have chores?
   - Should you have to wear your seat belt on the bus?
   - Should students who play sports still have to take gym class?
   - Should children be more concerned with what they eat so that they don't have health problems when they get older?
   - Should students get paid by their parents for getting good grades?
   - Should school be year-round with more breaks to improve education?
   - Do violent games and television shows make kids violent?
   - Should your school have a school newspaper?[1]

3. Collect the index cards and briefly look them over to make sure each one is an acceptable and argumentative topic.
4. Fold each index card and place it into a box (or other object from which you could draw the cards).
5. Explain to the class the rules of "Yes or No?" For each question that is drawn, students will stand on the side that matches their opinion. They will have 2 minutes to discuss their position with the group. Next, each side will have 2 minutes to present their side. Students will then be given 2 minutes to discuss their response to the information presented, followed by 2 minutes to respond. There will be three rounds until the next topic will be drawn, and the steps repeated.

6. It may be helpful to review "Accountable Talk" prior to this lesson. See Chapter 3 on mindfulness.

Distribute **Reproducible 6B1: "Yes or No?" Reflection Questions**.

Note

1 "20 Argumentative Essay Topics For Middle School." *It's Time to Learn More About Essay Writing*, Oxford University Summer School, oxforduniversitysummerschool.com/middle-school-argumentative-topics-20-excellent-prompts/.

7

Be Resilient

This chapter describes resiliency: the ability to recover from frustration or failure. This is one of the most desirable traits in the SEL pantheon. The critical first step in achieving resiliency is the ability to calm the mind when tempted to panic.

Why do some students handle anxiety so much better than others? While some researchers speculate that resilience is genetic and therefore an innate quality, several studies show that it can be cultivated.[1] Here are the main attributes (sometimes called "protective factors") that distinguish resilient people. They often:

- Perceive bad times only as temporary, and refrain from blaming themselves.
- Do not let hardships define them, and often set goals that inspire them to rise above painful obstacles or grief.
- Recognize their strengths.
- Challenge themselves to be honest.
- Respond actively and creatively to remain positive.
- Possess qualities that elicit positive reactions from those around them.
- Exhibit a high level of self-regulation.
- Reach out to an adult who can offer moral support.
- Have a special interest or talent, such as a knack for working with animals. Their interests absorb them and help to shelter them from negativity.

- Have superior intelligence and problem-solving skills.
- Elicit support, warmth, advice, and comfort from friends.
- Avoid association with delinquent peers.[2]

ESSENTIAL Questions

- How do people use different symbols to help them through challenging times?
- How can adopting a Growth Mindset improve our sense of self-efficacy?
- How can our attitudes about challenges in life affect how we cope with them? How can our attitudes sometimes affect the outcome of these challenges?

ACTIVITY 7A " 'Hope' Is the Thing With Feathers"

ELA Goal: Students will analyze the poem in terms of diction, figurative language, symbolism, and imagery.

SEL Goal—Self-Awareness: Students will develop self-awareness by describing a time in which they have faced adversity and identifying the thoughts, feelings, and actions that they experienced during this time. Students will also practice recognizing strengths they possess during these times and increase their sense of self-efficacy.

Materials Needed: Journals, **Reproducible 7A1: " 'Hope' Is the Thing With Feathers."**

" 'Hope' Is the Thing With Feathers"

Read the poem available here: www.poetryfoundation.org/poems/42889/hope-is-the-thing-with-feathers-314. Then answer the following questions.

Guided Reading Questions
1. In this poem, Emily Dickinson uses a metaphor for the idea of "Hope." What does she use to depict this idea? What specific words in the poem help you to identify this metaphor? 2. What do you think Dickinson means when she writes how "Hope . . . sings the tune without the words –/And never stops – at all –"? 3. When does "Hope" sound the "sweetest"? 4. Think about the type of weather that occurs during a "storm." What images do you see in your mind? What type of weather could she be describing here? 5. Thinking back to our journal prompt, let's connect the image of a "storm" to specific times in our lives. What could a "storm" represent when it relates to life? 6. When is it most important—and most difficult—to hear the "song" of "Hope"? 7. What do you think she means when she writes that "Hope" has "kept so many warm"? 8. What do you think she means when she writes how she has "heard ['Hope'] . . . in the chillest land –/And on the strangest Sea –"? Notice the contrast in temperatures here with the previous line of the poem. 9. Think about the word "adversity." How could times of adversity makes us feel "chill" and "strange"? 10. What do you think she means by the last two lines of the poem?

© 2019, Taylor & Francis, *Integrating SEL Into Your ELA Curriculum,*
John Dacey, Lindsey Neves Baillargeron, and Nancy Tripp

Journal Prompt for Quick-Write:

- What does the word "hope" mean to you? What comes to your mind when you think about this word?
- Describe a time in your life that has been particularly challenging for you. What happened? What made it challenging? How did you get through it?
- Why might it be important to have hope when we face challenging times in our lives? How can we have hope even when it may be very difficult?

PRE-READING Vocabulary

adversity (n.):   a difficult event or circumstance

perch (v.):[3]   to settle or rest in some elevated position

abash (v.):[4]   to destroy the self-confidence, poise, or self-possession of; disconcert; make ashamed or embarrassed

gale (n.):[5]   a very strong wind

sore (adj.):   sorrowful

extremity (n.):[6] the utmost or any extreme degree

Distribute **Reproducible 7A1: " 'Hope' Is the Thing With Feathers."**

ACTIVITY 7B The Crow and His Growth Mindset

ELA Goal: Identify conflict, character traits, and theme in a fable. Use evidence from the text to create a well-supported, coherent argument.

SEL Goal—Self-Awareness: Students will develop self-awareness by reflecting on a time in which they dealt with conflict. Students will develop an accurate self-perception and communication through journaling and class discussion. Lastly, students will improve their self-efficacy by learning about the Growth Mindset, as developed by Carol Dweck, and practicing applying it to their self-reflection.

Materials Needed: Journals, **Reproducible 7B1: "Self-Efficacy Assessment," Reproducible 7B2: "The Crow and His Growth Mindset," Reproducible 7B3: Growth Mindset Model, Reproducible 7B4: Growth Mindset Practice**.

"Self-Efficacy Assessment"

self-efficacy: (n.) a person's belief in how well he/she can succeed in accomplishing a specific goal or task[7]

On a scale of 1–5, how would you rate your level of self-efficacy?
1: I never feel like I will successfully achieve my goals.
2: I sometimes feel like I will successfully achieve my goals.
3: I usually feel like I will successfully achieve my goals.
4: I most often feel like I will successfully achieve my goals.
5: I always feel like I will successfully achieve my goals.

"The Crow and His Growth Mindset"

By Aesop, Eliot/Jacobs version

A Crow, half-dead with thirst, came upon a Pitcher which had once been full of water; but when the Crow put its beak into the mouth of the Pitcher he found that only very little water was left in it, and that he could not reach far enough down to get at it. He tried, and he tried, but at last had to give up in despair.

Then a thought came to him, and he took a pebble and dropped it into the Pitcher. Then he took another pebble and dropped it into the Pitcher. Then he took another pebble and dropped that into the Pitcher. Then he took another pebble and dropped that into the Pitcher. Then he took another pebble and dropped that into the Pitcher. Then he took another pebble and dropped that into the Pitcher. At last, at last, he saw the water mount up near him, and after casting in a few more pebbles he was able to quench his thirst and save his life.

Review conflict in literature:

Internal: character vs. self
External: character vs. nature, character vs. society, character vs. character, character vs. object
Conflict is what drives the plot of a story.

Discussion questions:

1. What is the main conflict in the story?
2. What type of conflict is it? Why?
3. What is the moral of the story?
4. What character traits describe the crow?
5. How does the crow demonstrate self-efficacy?

Growth Mindset Model

Fixed Mindset vs. Growth Mindset[8]

Fixed Mindset	Growth Mindset
"I'm just not good at this." "I'll never be able to do this."	"I haven't figured out what works yet." "If I keep trying a different way, I will most likely find a solution."
"This is not what I expected would happen. Everything is ruined!" "This is too hard. I'm just going to try and avoid it." "I'm not going to get it right. Why even bother?"	"While this was not the situation I expected, I can see it as an opportunity for learning and growth." "The best way to improve is to face challenges head-on." "Anything worth doing is hard work."

Growth Mindset Practice

Practice Activity:

How does the crow display a growth mindset in this story?

Think of a time recently in which your thoughts resembled those of a fixed mindset. Write them in the left-hand column, then try to revise them so they show the perspective of a growth mindset.

Fixed Mindset	Growth Mindset
1.	1.
2.	2.
3.	3.

- Ask the students to reflect on their self-assessment. Revisit this assessment at the conclusion of the class discussion on the fable.

Journal prompt: Describe a time in which you struggled to find a solution for a problem you were having. It could be a question on a test, a conflict/argument you were having with a friend or family member, or a strategy in a sports game. Reflect on these questions:

- What was the problem you faced?
- What was your attitude like when you approached the problem? Did you feel like you could find a solution, did you have thoughts of self-doubt, or perhaps a little bit of both?
- What did you do about it?
- What was the outcome?

Distribute **Reproducible 7B1: "Self-Efficacy Assessment," Reproducible 7B2: "The Crow and His Growth Mindset," Reproducible 7B3: Growth Mindset Model,** and **Reproducible 7B4: Growth Mindset Practice**.

Share answers on **Reproducible 7B4: Growth Mindset Practice** in partners/small groups. Discuss similarities and offer new ways to revise the growth mindset side, then share out as a class.

Journal Reflection:

Now reflect on a time in which you struggled and didn't achieve your goals. Think about the way you approached the task. Could you perhaps have approached it differently? What other strategies could you perhaps have used? If you had a chance to go back in time, what would you do differently?

Exit Slip:

What is your most important "take-away" from today's lesson? What is self-efficacy?

ACTIVITY 7C Becoming "Invictus"

ELA Goal: Students will be able to comprehend and define important vocabulary words from the poem "Invictus." Students will practice close reading and analyze figurative language, mood, and tone in the poem.

SEL Goal—Self-Awareness: Students will practice perspective-taking through poetry analysis, work on recognizing strengths, improving self-confidence, and enhancing their self-efficacy.

Self-Management: Students will also discuss ways to improve self-discipline, self-motivation, and goal setting.

Materials Needed: Journals, **Reproducible 7C1: Becoming "Invictus,"** **Reproducible 7C2: Looking Deeply at "Invictus."**

Becoming "Invictus"

Read the poem together (modified version offered on right for students who need modifications):

Invictus	"Invictus": Modified
Out of the night that covers me, Black as the pit from pole to pole, I thank whatever gods may be For my unconquerable soul.	*Out of the night that covers me,*
	Where my whole world feels like a dark pit
	I thank whatever gods may be,
	For my unconquerable soul.
In the fell clutch of circumstance I have not winced nor cried aloud. Under the bludgeonings of chance My head is bloody, but unbowed.	*During times when things don't go my way*
	I have not winced nor cried aloud.
	When life presents me with an unfortunate situation
	My head is bloody, but unbowed.
Beyond this place of wrath and tears Looms but the Horror of the shade, And yet the menace of the years Finds and shall find me unafraid.	*Beyond this dark and difficult place where I cry tears*
	I may feel my fear of death
	And yet the evil of the years
	Finds and will always find me unafraid
It matters not how strait the gate, How charged with punishments the scroll, I am the master of my fate, I am the captain of my soul.	*It doesn't matter how difficult the obstacle,*
	Or how long the list of challenges I face,
	I am the master of my fate,
	I am the captain of my soul.

Inferential questions (to be answered in small groups):

1. In the first line of the poem, the poet uses a metaphor. Identify the metaphor. What could this metaphor represent?
2. What kind of mood does the first stanza establish for the reader?
3. In the second stanza, the poet uses two examples of alliteration. Write the two examples below.
4. How does the poet's use of alliteration help you to focus on important images in the poem? What do you think these images mean?
5. After reading the third stanza, what impression do you get of the speaker's life? What has his life been like so far? What lines specifically suggest your interpretation?
6. Read the last two lines of the poem. What is the speaker's attitude toward the challenges he has faced? How do you think he will face challenges in his future?

Looking Closely at "Invictus"

Text Rendering Experience[9]

Roles:

A facilitator to lead the small group discussion.
A scribe to write down the phrases and words that are shared.

Activity:

Take a few moments to review the poem and underline the line, the phrase, and the word that you think is particularly meaningful in this piece of literature.

Steps:

1. First round: Each person shares a sentence from the poem that he/she thinks/feels is particularly vivid/important/meaningful.
2. Second round: Each person shares a phrase that he/she thinks/feels is particularly vivid/important/meaningful. The scribe writes down each phrase.
3. Third round: Each person shares the word that he/she thinks/feels is particularly vivid/important/meaningful. The scribe records each word.
4. The group discusses what they heard and what it says about the poem. The group can discuss poetic elements, e.g., mood, tone, theme, a conflict that the speaker is experiencing, and/or the overall meaning of the poem.
5. The group shares any new insights they have gained about the poem after discussing it with their small groups.

PRE-READING Vocabulary

Invictus (from Latin):   unconquered

pit (n.):   a large, deep hole in the ground

unconquerable (adj.):   unable to be defeated

clutch (n.):   tight grip

winced (v.):   to flinch, as in pain

bludgeonings (n.):   heavy beatings, as with a club

unbowed (adj.):   not defeated

wrath (n.):   punishment

looms (v.):   waits

menace (n.):   evil

strait (adj.):   narrow, difficult

Pre-reading vocabulary challenge: Students work in pairs to write a paragraph that contains as many words from the list as they can. Words must be used correctly. Variation: Students write a sentence for each word—this could be assigned as homework the night before reading the poem in class.

Distribute **Reproducible 7C1: Becoming "Invictus"** and **Reproducible 7C2: Looking Deeply at "Invictus."**

ACTIVITY 7D Empowerment Through Poetry

ELA Goal: Students analyze the poem "It Couldn't Be Done" in terms of characterization, tone, and theme.

SEL Goal—Self-Awareness: Students will work on recognizing strengths, improving self-confidence, and enhancing their self-efficacy.

Self-Management: Students will also discuss ways to improve self-discipline, self-motivation, and goal setting.

Materials Needed: Journals, **Reproducible 7D1: "It Couldn't Be Done."**

"It Couldn't Be Done"

It Couldn't Be Done By Edgar Albert Guest	Poetry Annotations

Somebody said that it couldn't be done,
 	
    But he with a chuckle replied
 	
That "maybe it couldn't," but he would be one
 	
    Who wouldn't say so till he'd tried.
 	
So he buckled right in with the trace of a grin
 	
    On his face. If he worried he hid it.
 	
He started to sing as he tackled the thing
 	
    That couldn't be done, and he did it.
 	
Somebody scoffed: "Oh, you'll never do that;
 	
    At least no one ever has done it";
 	
But he took off his coat and he took off his hat,
 	
    And the first thing we knew he'd begun it.
 	
With a lift of his chin and a bit of a grin,
 	
    Without any doubting or quiddit,
 	
He started to sing as he tackled the thing
 	
    That couldn't be done, and he did it.
	_____
	
	_____
	
	_____
	
	_____
	
	_____
	
	_____
	
	_____
	
	_____
	
	_____
	
	_____
	
	_____
	
	_____
	
	_____
	
	_____
	
	_____
	
	_____
	
	_____
	
	_____

There are thousands to tell you it cannot be done,

    There are thousands to prophesy failure;

There are thousands to point out to you one by one,

    The dangers that wait to assail you.

But just buckle in with a bit of a grin,

    Just take off your coat and go to it;

Just start in to sing as you tackle the thing

    That "cannot be done," and you'll do it.

_____

_____

_____

_____

_____

_____

_____

_____

_____

Guiding Questions

1. What is the conflict that the poet presents in this poem?
2. What character traits would you use to describe the subject of this poem? How did he respond to the conflict? Use two lines from the text to support your answer.
3. How would you describe the subject's attitude? What lines in the poem lead you to think this way?
4. What is the message of the poem? What lines in the poem lead you to think this way?

Journal Prompt

- Describe a time when you attempted something that, at first, you thought you couldn't do—or something that someone else thought you couldn't do.
- What did you do? How did you do it?
- What thoughts went through your mind at the time?
- How did you overcome any thoughts of self-doubt you might have had?

Distribute **Reproducible 7D1: "It Couldn't Be Done."**

Extended Practice Activities:

#1: Create a comic strip illustrating this poem. Use your close reading of the poem to create your illustrations.

Next, imagine *yourself* in the poem, facing something that is difficult *for you*. Visualize a similar progression of events in your mind. Complete the comic strip, illustrating yourself with similar character traits, a similar attitude, and a similar outcome as the subject in this poem.

#2: Imagine that you have a friend that is struggling to do something that he/she thinks he/she cannot do. Maybe he/she is thinking about trying out for the basketball team, making a new friend, trying a new hobby, or moving to a new school. Write a letter using this poem as inspiration, encouraging your friend to take a risk, have courage, and try despite having thoughts of self-doubt. Consider giving it to your friend to give them a bit of encouragement!

Notes

1 Bethell, 2014.
2 Masten, 2014.
3 "Perch." *Dictionary.com Unabridged*. Random House, Inc. January 20, 2018.
4 "Abash." *Dictionary.com Unabridged*. Random House, Inc. January 20, 2018.
5 "Gale." *Dictionary.com Unabridged*. Random House, Inc. January 20, 2018.
6 "Extremity." *Dictionary.com Unabridged*. Random House, Inc. January 20, 2018.
7 Bandura, 1994.
8 Dweck, 2006.
9 Adapted from "Text Rendering Experience." *National School Reform Faculty*, Harmony Education Center, 2014.

Part III

Social Awareness

8

Cooperate and Compete Successfully

A teacher stood at her classroom window on a cold, rainy November afternoon. She could see the football team doing calisthenics. Most of the players were smiling, and all were enthusiastic. "We need that kind of motivation in here," she thought. "What makes playing football so much more valuable to them?"

Immediately the answer came to her:

- There is great joy in working together as a team for a common goal.
- The common goal is to win in competition against other teams.

Why not in the classroom, she wondered? As you undoubtedly know, this creative concept has not swept the world of education. Why not?[1]

Competition is everywhere. We are constantly being encouraged to compare ourselves to others. In fact, evolution programmed it into our genes.[2] Schools are rated on their test scores, colleges on their graduates' success, teams on their win/loss records. Employees are rewarded with higher salaries and promotions, beauty pageant contestants by winning Miss Whatever (or the always-dreaded Miss Congeniality).

Clearly, there are situations in which competition provides the best motivation, However, educational research suggests that students do better when they work cooperatively.[3] Far from "survival of the fittest," the human story could be titled "survival of the most connected." This is true for families, neighborhoods, and nations.[4] And SEL can help. Here are strategies for fostering each of them.

ACTIVITY 8A Sentenced to Win

ELA Goal: Using cooperative skills to achieve correct sentence structure.

SEL Goal—Social Awareness: Develop core skills of communication and perspective-taking, and as well as conflict resolution, both internal and external.

Materials Needed: None.

Tell students that to be successful in this activity, they will need to control their emotions (see Chapter 4). To win, they are going to have to think fast, but not so fast that they lose concentration. They will be working together in groups of three to make up two sentences. In the first round, they should use the following words to make up a complete, grammatically correct sentence: **prime, apples, nosy, fish**, and **correction**. For example, their sentence might be, "The old lady sold apples and fish from her cart, but her prime motive was to offer people correction because she was so nosy." Not a great sentence, but one that is grammatically correct.

In the second round, producing the second sentence, students should use the following words: **cake, mission, cell phone, park**, and **peak**. The first group to form a reasonable sentence in each round wins that round.

Now ask the groups to work together to answer the following questions:

- If your group was first to form one of the sentences, why do you think you were successful?
- If you lost, why did you lose? If your group was not among either of the two winners, what was your group's problem? What can you tell me about your group's communication skills?
- Which was most important in being successful: cooperation or competition?

ACTIVITY 8B Where's Your Strength?

ELA Goal: Use established criteria to review a peer's writing, and draw conclusions based on evidence.

SEL Goal—Self-Awareness/Responsible Decision-Making: Learn to use criteria to rate one's self, and to apply those judgments in real situations.

Materials Needed: **Reproducible 8B1: Data Recording Sheet.**

Data Recording Sheet

Activity	Above average	Average	Below average	Teacher rate; 0 (average), + or–
Topic Introduction				
Research				
Transitions to Create Cohesion				
Persuasion				
Support for Claims				
Grammar				
Clarity				
Cohesion				
Use of Graphics (e.g., charts, tables)				
Overall Writing				

Pass out **Reproducible 8B1: Data Recording Sheet**. Ask your students to think about the ELA activities on this form and how well they think they are able to practice them. (On the blank rows, add any other abilities you would like to rate.)

Explain what you mean by of the writing activities, and as you explain each one, tell your students that for this skill, they should check the choice next to it that best describes how capable they are in that trait: below average, average, above average. Collect the papers and when you have time, rate each of their abilities (zero equals agree, plus equals more skilled than they think they are, and minus equals less skilled than they think they are).

Tell them to pick one ELA skill that they think they are better at than you do, and ask them to prove it. That is, if they think their writing has more clarity than you do, ask them to try to convince you of that by writing a passage that shows a high level of clarity.

ACTIVITY 8C Being a Good Sport

ELA Goal: Learn to express oneself with clear and concise language, appropriate to task and audience.

SEL Goal—Responsible Decision-Making: Learning to gain control over contradictory feelings when competing.

Materials Needed: **Reproducible 8C1: Questions** (a set of 10 questions that can easily be answered by middle-schoolers).

Questions

1. "What is the date today?"

2. "How many kids are in your group?"

3. "What is your teacher's last name?"

4. "What is the principal's last name?"

5. "What is the name of our school?"

6. "What part of our country is the state in?"

7. "How much is $2 + 3 + 6$?"

8. "What is the capital of our state?"

9. "About how old is the average student in this class?"

10. "In what section of the building is our classroom situated?"

Ask your students if they have ever met anyone who is just naturally a good sport. These would be individuals who never get mad at other people or at themselves when they lose. Tell them you never have, either! This is probably because of the Dunning-Kruger effect,[5] which is "the tendency of unskilled individuals to believe their abilities are better than they really are."

Divide the class into two equal groups with one group sitting on the left of the room and one group sitting on the right. Explain the rules of the game to the students. You will start questioning those on the left first. If they get the correct answer, they get 1 point. If they don't, you will ask the same question to the students on the right, and if they get the correct answer, they will get 2 points. Ready?

Begin asking your questions (**Reproducible 8C1**), and keep a record of the score of the group on the left. You can be confident that pretty soon, the group on the right will start to complain: "Hey, that's not fair!" "The questions you're giving them are too easy!" "They're cheating, we don't have a chance!" "Why should you treat them special? There is nothing special about them!"

Now say to the children on the right, "Okay, you are correct, this game was not fair. You never had a chance to score points because the questions were too easy and the other group got all of them right. I can understand why you got upset. However, suppose you were trying to be a good sport about it. What would you have said instead?"

The children will probably say things like, "Congratulations, you won!" or "You guys did a nice job!" Now ask the group who won the contest.

- "How did it feel when someone accused you of being cheaters?"
- "Was it better when they said, 'Nice job,' even though you knew you only won because the questions were so easy?"

Now some questions for the whole class:

- "How can we decide what is fair and what is unfair?"
- "Can you think of any time when you have been a good sport?"
- "What helps you to be more cooperative and less competitive?"

Educational Equity

This last activity is about fairness, but it also touches on the concept of educational equity, which is defined as follows:

[It] implies that all students have access to the resources and educational rigor they need despite race, gender, ethnicity, language, disability, family background, or family income. Striving for educational equity encourages educators to examine biases and create inclusive, multicultural school environments.[6]

What are the implications of SEL for educational equity? In his CASEL webinar on the subject, educator Robert Jagers identified the following elements for each of the five types of SEL. Please study them. It is beyond the scope of this book to go into them in detail, but we hope you can see that these concepts have many implications for promoting SEL.

Implications of Educational Equity for Promoting SEL

1. Self-awareness

   Examining the importance of various social identities
   Deriving constructive meanings of social identities
   Grounding in and affirming of cultural heritage(s)

2. Self-management

   Coping with acculturative stress
   Coping with discrimination/prejudice

3. Social awareness

   Discerning the importance of diversity (situational)
   Understanding the meaning of diversity in contexts (climate)
   Recognizing cultural demands and opportunities
   Collective efficacy

4. Relationship skills

   Demonstrating cultural competence
   Leveraging cultural fluency

5. Responsible decision-making

   Considering diversity salience and climate
   Assessing the impact of one's beliefs and biases
   Pursuing inclusive, mutually beneficial solutions
   Reflecting on the broader ethical consequences of one's decisions for intragroup, intergroup, and institutional relations.[7]

As you attempt to teach SEL concepts as they relate to competition and cooperation, please try to keep as many of these factors as possible in mind.

ACTIVITY 8D Look, Mom, No Hands!

ELA Goal: Write informative/explanatory texts, including the narration of scientific procedures/experiments

SEL Goal—Relationship Skills: Develop interpersonal cooperation skills.

Materials Needed: Six empty cans (soda, soup, etc.; have some students bring them in). One 10-inch string (could also be a strong rubber band) with four "handles" attached to it. The handles are four pieces of string, each 6 inches long. See **Reproducible 8D1: Cooperative Can Mover, Reproducible 8D2: Empty Cans, Loose, and Stacked**.

This activity would work well as an interdiscplinary/co-teaching lesson with a science teacher.

Cooperative Can Mover

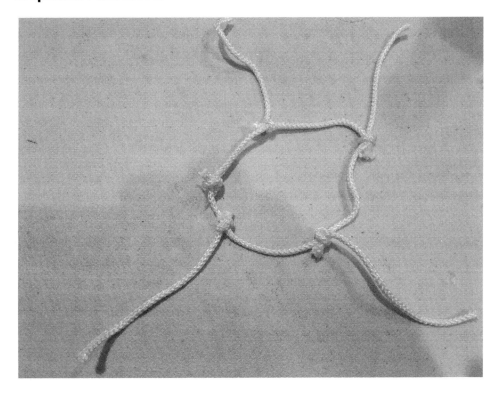

You needn't show the photo to students unless you'd like them to construct their own. You could make one for each team of five in your class, if you want.

Empty Cans, Loose, and Stacked

Tell students that their goal is to create a tower with their six empty cans—three on the bottom row, two on the second and one on the top (see **Reproducible 8D2: Empty Cans, Loose, and Stacked**). To make the tower they need to work together using ONLY using the string tool. They need to work together to pick up and place one can at a time without talking. Tell them they must coordinate their work silently.

They should decide which four of the five students will form the can-moving team. The fifth student will be the recorder and will take notes on the process the others employ. Each member of the team is to pull on one of the strings, until the circular string is stretched into a square large enough to fit over a can. (Note: If a can turns over or rolls off the table, participants can pick it up and place it back on the table. Other than that, no touching!) If they succeed quickly, they can create variations: add more cans, turn the top can upside down, set a time limit, and so forth.

When each team of five students have had a try, ask them to gather and discuss their results. Have the recorders report on what kinds of problems the teams encountered. Use the following questions:

- What was fun?
- What was frustrating?
- What skills did they need in order to succeed? (Examples include non-verbal communication, coordination, patience, willingness to follow a leader.)
- How did they manage to communicate so they could work together?
- How do these skills help people get along or succeed in life? In your family? In our classroom or school?

ACTIVITY 8E My Worst Fear

ELA Goal: Develop a topic with relevant, well-chosen facts, definitions, concrete details, quotations, or other information and examples.

SEL Goal—Social Awareness

Materials Needed: **Reproducible 8E1: Short Story Introductory Paragraph, from *The Telltale Heart* by Edgar Allan Poe, Reproducible 8E2: Examples of Good Writing.**

Short Story Introductory Paragraph, From *The Telltale Heart* by Edgar Allan Poe

TRUE! NERVOUS—very, very dreadfully nervous I had been and am! But why *will* you say that I am mad? The disease had sharpened my senses—not destroyed—not dulled them. Above all things was the sense of hearing acute. I heard all things in the heaven and in the earth. I heard many things in hell. How, then, am I mad? Hearken! and observe how healthily—how calmly I can tell you the whole story.

Examples of Good Writing

Type of Good Writing	Examples of Good Writing
Relevant, Well-Chosen Facts	
Concrete Details	
Quotations	
Other Information and Examples	

Ask students to read **Reproducible 8E1** and discuss in small groups what techniques Poe has used: relevant, well-chosen facts, definitions, concrete details, and other information. Then they are to write the scariest story they can, in one to two pages. When most students have finished, to their small groups. As each student reads his brief story (SLOWLY), ask the other two to fill out **Reproducible 8E2** with examples of the reader's writing. Finally, ask each small group to discuss how each of the short stories would be improved by adding elements of the **Examples of Good Writing** listed in **Reproducible 8E2**.

Notes

1 Coleman, 1969.
2 Das, 2013.
3 Cohen, 2001; Slavin, 2013; Johnson, Johnson, & Stamme, 2000.
4 Rifkin, 2009.
5 Wikipedia, 2018.
6 Jagers, 2018.
7 Jagers, 2018, p. 1.

9

Neither a Bully Nor Bullied

Teachers know they must constantly be alert to bullying and be proactive in giving students strategies to recognize and deal with it. Moms Fight Back, an anti-bullying organization, reports that "74 percent of eight- to 11-year-olds say teasing and bullying happen at their school, and 15% of high school students report experiencing cyberbullying in the past year." Victims of bullying, the bullies themselves, and even those children who simply witness bullying will struggle in school and sometimes stop attending out of fear, experience low self-esteem, live in a constant state of stress response, become depressed, and often turn to violence themselves. The American Academy of Child and Adolescent Psychiatry states that "close to half of all children will experience school bullying at some point while they are at primary or secondary school."[1] Many others, obviously, will do the bullying.

Many state and local governments have stepped in to create laws around bullying. Although legislation is absolutely critical to enforce policies that will affect children, it's sometimes difficult to identify the players in the bullying cycle. The terms "bully," "victim," and "bystander" are commonly used to describe what takes place. Researchers note that many bullies have been victims of bullying themselves and, therefore, continue a destructive cycle.

Schools and other organizations have developed creative ways to break the cycle of bullying and to foster a more positive culture where bullying is incompatible with school norms.

An insightful statement from a high school student, written in a recent *Huffington Post Teen* online article, is worth sharing here: "Up until now, our society has been trying to reform bullies while treating victims as martyrs.

By focusing on bullies, we have actually given them more power. Instead, we need to shift our focus away from bullying behaviors and concentrate on building the inner strength of all students."[2]

Teamwork, conflict resolution, trust-building, service learning, encouraging group identity, and cooperation and competition are but a few of the complex strategies now being attempted. Successful anti-bullying typically attempt to build greater capacity for empathy, which has a direct link to bullying.[3] As discussed in Chapter 3, mindfulness practices (e.g., meditation, centering) build values that are more empathetic and help encourage connectedness and perspective-taking, as well as improve concentration.[4] Similarly, increasing independent thinking, as described in Chapter 6, prepares students to both stand up to bullies and resist the temptation to bully others.

When children are in groups, subtler forms of mistreatment (e.g., shunning) can be as devastating. These understated forms of bullying often tend to occur in smaller schools or in classrooms with fewer children. The following activities prevent bullying by helping students to develop greater empathy, respect for one another, conflict resolution, and healthy ways to work together.

ACTIVITY 9A Trust Walk

ELA Goal: Students will be able to identify the mood in a particular real-life scenario and explain the mood with clear and concise language appropriate to purpose and audience.

SEL Goal—Relationship Skills: Help children experience vulnerability in a safe, controlled environment.

Materials Needed: A blindfold, bandana, or scarf.

Remind students that people are animals, and as animals we use our senses to navigate the world around us. Have students make a list of how humans and other animals may use their senses. Tell them that when one sense is limited or not available, animals typically strengthen another sense to use in its place. In the trust walk, they will experience their environment without their sense of sight, the sense they rely on the most. Explain that this will make them vulnerable and that vulnerability will push them to rely more on their other senses, for as well as the help of a classmate.

This activity would work well as a team-building exercise.

Invite students to pair up in teams of one boy and one girl. Ask them to decide who will be the first with her[5] eyes closed, and who will be the guide. Say, "We're going to take a walk together. On this walk, one person will have her eyes covered, and one person will be the guide. It is the guide's job to make sure that the person with her eyes blinded is safe. This means making sure that no one bumps into anything, trips over anything, or falls or stubs toes. When you are the guide, you should make the walk as interesting as possible for your partner. You may go up or down stairs, and enter rooms with different sounds or smells. As you're walking, touch different objects or feel different textures on the walls or floors. Take this trust walk silently. Try to be quiet the entire time. Use your imagination only. When I tell you, you will stop wherever you are and switch roles—the guides will put on the blindfolds and those who were blindfolded will now be the guides."

When the children have completed their turns as guides and "trustees," they may discuss as a class the following questions:

- How did it feel to have your eyes closed and to rely on your partner?
- Did you feel more comfortable blindfolded or as the guide?
- Did you enjoy the trust walk? What did you like most about it?
- What would you change next time?
- Has doing this activity changed you for the better? For example, do you feel more trusting of each other?

Finally, they should work together in groups of two boys and two girls generate a web or two column notes to organize their thinking. At the bottom of their two-column notes, summarize what individuals said about how they felt and what they observed during the exercise (use two-column note template with summary at the bottom). Write a reflection in their reader/writer's notebooks of what they learned from this experience.

ACTIVITY 9B The Conflict Within

ELA Goal: All good stories involve a series of events: the plot that involves a problem. Learning how the problem is typically related to a number of choices or decisions a character in the story makes is a significant goal of middle school ELA instruction.

SEL Goal—Self-Awareness and Responsible Decision-Making: To help students recognize internal conflicts they may be experiencing, and to notice how these conflicts affect them and others.

Materials Needed: Pencils, crayons, colored pencils for drawing.

Ask each students to think about some choices they have made recently— today, yesterday, this week, or even this month. How did these decisions arise from a conflict they were experiencing? With whom do they most often get into conflict? For example, which acquaintance would be most likely to cause a problem if invited to their birthday party? We sometimes find our- selves thinking about whether a choice that we made is in sync with our val- ues. How do we think we are supposed to act? Ask what decision they might make that would most likely lead to their being bullied. Create a storyboard to illustrate the events, or use a plot chart to map the events including the conflict in the middle. To extend this, you might ask them to write a one-page story depicting this conflict.

Now ask your pupils to describe in writing three difficult choices they had to make recently. Which decisions do they feel good about and which ones do they wish they could do over? Did the decisions result in conflict? If so, were they able to resolve those conflicts? How?

ACTIVITY 9C On a Deserted Island I Would Bring . . .

ELA Goal: Distinguish one's own point of view from that of others.

SEL Goal—Responsible Decision-Making: To help children recognize different strengths in others and how they might better appreciate those strengths.

Materials Needed: Index cards or small pieces of paper to write on, pencils.

Explain to the class that they are all a mix of strengths and challenges, and that understanding those traits will help them to make good decisions about their pursuits and interests. Ask students to form small groups and make a list of strengths and challenges that children in their grade might have. Explain further how point of view and context affect whether we see a trait as positive or negative. A perceived strength from one point of view may be considered a challenge by another, or in a different situation. For example, sincere honesty may clear the air, or it may make things exceedingly tense.

Tell students that they're going to pretend that they are heading to a deserted island for a short stay. Ask students to consider what kind of person would be most helpful to travel with. Then ask them to describe the ideal person they would want to travel with by listing advantageous traits on an index card/piece of paper. For example, a student might say, "I want someone who knows how to cook," or she might say, "I would want someone funny to make me laugh while we're there." Ask students to share their answers with each other. Then make a request of several students: "Please read some of the positive traits you wrote on your index cards." Ask the class which characteristics were listed the most? The least?

Ask students to highlight traits that would be helpful on the deserted island, but seen as not helpful at a birthday party. Examples: the ability to find water; the skill of spear-throwing. Then say that we have to recognize that our own strengths and challenges and those of others may be helpful and valued in some circumstances, but not in others. In fact, some traits may even be seen as bullying! Ask the class to think of some examples. Ask students examples of someone judging, teasing, or bullying someone else because that person had a misperception of that first person's intentions.

ACTIVITY 9D Tower of Cards

ELA Goal: Plan and carry out research to answer a question or test a theory.

SEL Goal—Relationship Skills: Help children work together to create and complete a collaborative project, which requires listening to and acknowledging others' ideas.

Materials Needed: Sets of 30 index cards, one pair of scissors for each group.

Say to students that they're going to work in small groups for this activity. Note that teamwork isn't always easy and often requires people to share ideas, listen to one another, create, and compromise. Mention that they've got a package of index cards and a pair of scissors they can use to create a tower. It should be a special tower, unlike any of the others would come up with. They may use the scissors to alter the cards in any way they like. The rules are that each group member gets a chance to participate in the creation, and each teammate helps to decide what that creation will be. Give the players 15 minutes to work with the index cards. When they are finished, invite them to examine the creations that others came up with.

Encourage students to share their ideas and processes with the other children in the class. Some questions for discussion are:

- Why did you decide to create your final product the way you did?
- Did you have any problems coming up with an idea for your creation? Did you have any problems working together to make it?
- Did anyone try to be the boss of the project?

- How did you negotiate about how to work together?
- What would you do differently next time?

This activity would work well as an interdisciplinary exercise with a science, mathematics, or engineering teacher.

Notes

1 AACAP, 2011, p. 1.
2 Huang & Cornell, 2015
3 Van Noorden, 2016.
4 English, 2014.
5 Remember, we use the female pronoun here only because this is in that chapter, not because we think girls should go first.

Part IV

Relationship Skills

10

Develop Fruitful Friendships

There is something deeply elementary about the desire to be connected to others and to feel that others wish to connect with us.[1] This mutually reciprocal linking is known by different names, but for our purposes, we will focus on friendships. Our need for attachment has contributed to the rise in social media usage among children and teens, and in the age of the "selfie," children thinking about others as much as themselves seems strange.

Teaching and strengthening the qualities and attributes of friendship is both possible and positive. Research shows that when we think about other people, our minds actually expand.[2] There are portions of our brain that respond when we think kind, compassionate thoughts, and over time—like any exercise—we can strengthen these parts of our brain and contribute to a happier, healthier society at the same time.

Often, when people reflect on their own capacity to behave in a compassionate manner, they face dilemmas. One is that empathy is rarely taught explicitly at home or at school because it is often "considered intuitive and therefore difficult to teach, or a 'soft' emotional skill."[3] So by explicitly teaching, modeling, and providing opportunities to practice empathy, we teach students to be empathetic by stepping into each other's experiences.

In his brilliant book, *Childhood and Society*, Erikson speaks of "validation," which works in two steps. First we reveal, usually in the form of a confession, something about ourselves to someone in whom we have placed our trust—a friend. This is always a risky proposition, because the friend could easily invalidate our sense of identity by expressing their disgust. Suppose for example, a student confesses to a friend that he never watches television.

If that friend responds by saying, "You never watch TV? That's weird!," the integration of the confessor's psyche is likely to fracture. Now suppose on the other hand, that friend says, "Yeah, I don't spend my time watching TV either." Then the friend goes on to describe the specifics of his own experience, and by this admission, makes himself vulnerable. This friend's approval, followed by his trustful description of his own self-doubting action, is what Erikson means by validation. Elements such as validation, compassion, and empathy, coupled with kindness and respect for the challenges of others, are the foundation of good friendships.

ESSENTIAL Questions

- How do friendships help us to lead happy and healthy lives?
- What qualities does a good friend possess?
- How can collaboration with others help us to face and overcome obstacles in our lives?
- How can literature and writing teach us how to address conflicts in friendships?
- Who is a true friend?

ACTIVITY 10A "A Time to Talk"

ELA Goal: Students will analyze the poem "A Time to Talk" in terms of imagery, diction, and theme.

SEL Goal—Social Awareness: Students will practice perspective-taking through literary analysis and work on developing relationship skills, especially related to communication, social engagement and relationship building.

Materials Needed: **Reproducible 10A1: "A Time to Talk,"** blank piece of paper to use as drawing paper.

"A Time to Talk"

Read the poem found here: www.bartleby.com/119/14.html

Annotate it line by line using the following chart.

Poetry Annotations

Journal Prompt for Quick-Write: Why is it important to spend time with our friends?

PRE-READING Vocabulary

hoe (n.): a tool with a long handle that is used to break up soil in the ground

mellow (adj.): (in the context of this poem) softened—as in softened ground

plod (v.): to walk at a slow pace

Optional: Have students illustrate what they see in their minds while listening to the poem.

Distribute **Reproducible 10A1: "A Time to Talk."** Ask students to answer the following questions in small groups:

- What is the speaker doing at the beginning of the poem?
- What happens that causes him to stop what he is doing?
- Why do you think he decides to stop what he is doing and "go up to the stone wall/For a friendly visit"?

INFERENTIAL Questions

- Why is the poem called "A Time to Talk"? What is another title he could have used for this poem?
- What does he mean when he says: "I don't stand still and look around/On all the hills I haven't hoed,/And shout from where I am, 'What is it?'"
- In this poem, the speaker sets his tool aside. While he *literally* sets this tool aside, what does he also *figuratively* set aside?
- How do you think the speaker's decision to spend time talking with his friend will help strengthen their friendship?
- What is the theme/message in this poem? What do you think Frost would like readers to take away or learn from reading this poem?
- Do you agree with his message? Why or why not?

ACTIVITY 10B The Fox and the Horse

ELA Goal: Students will identify the conflict in the story and evaluate how friendship helped the characters to resolve the conflict.

Students will describe the fox and the horse using character traits, supporting their claim with evidence from the folktale.

SEL Goal—Social Awareness, Relationships, and Responsible Decision-Making: Students will understand the importance of empathy and "reading" another person's needs, the power of communication and teamwork, and the benefits that come with working together to identify, analyze, and solve problems.

Materials Needed: Journal or notebook, **Reproducible 10B1: "The Fox and the Horse," Reproducible 10B2: Understanding Plot in a Fable**.

"The Fox and the Horse"

By Jacob and Wilhelm Grimm

A peasant had a faithful horse which had grown old and could do no more work, so his master no longer wanted to give him anything to eat and said, "I can certainly make no more use of you, but still I mean well by you, and if you prove yourself still strong enough to bring me a lion here, I will maintain you. But for now get out of my stable." And with that he chased him into the open field.

The horse was sad, and went to the forest to seek a little protection there from the weather. There the fox met him and said, "Why do you hang your head so, and go about all alone?"

"Alas," replied the horse, "greed and loyalty do not dwell together in one house. My master has forgotten what services I have performed for him for so many years, and because I can no longer plow well, he will give me no more food, and has driven me out."

"Without giving you a chance?" asked the fox.

"The chance was a bad one. He said, if I were still strong enough to bring him a lion, he would keep me, but he well knows that I cannot do that."

The fox said, "I will help you. Just lie down, stretch out as if you were dead, and do not stir."

The horse did what the fox asked, and then the fox went to the lion, who had his den not far off, and said, "A dead horse is lying out there. Just come with me, and you can have a rich meal."

The lion went with him, and when they were both standing by the horse the fox said, "After all, it is not very comfortable for you here—I tell you what—I will fasten it to you by the tail, and then you can drag it into your cave and eat it in peace."

This advice pleased the lion. He positioned himself, and in order that the fox might tie the horse fast to him, he kept completely quiet. But the fox tied the lion's legs together with the horse's tail, and twisted and fastened everything so well and so strongly that no amount of strength could pull it loose. When he had finished his work, he tapped the horse on the shoulder and said, "Pull, white horse, pull!"

Then up sprang the horse at once, and pulled the lion away with him. The lion began to roar so that all the birds in the forest flew up in terror, but the horse let him roar, and drew him and dragged him across the field to his master's door. When the master saw the lion, he was of a better mind, and said to the horse, "You shall stay with me and fare well." And he gave him plenty to eat until he died.[4]

Understanding Plot in a Fable

Create a plot diagram of the story.

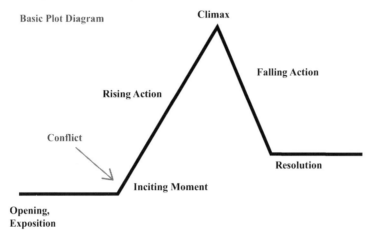

Journal Prompt Quick-Write: Describe a time when you helped a friend in need, or when a friend helped you when you were in need, when a friend helped you to solve a problem, or when you helped your friend to solve a problem.

PRE-READING Vocabulary

solitary (adj.):   alone

avarice (n.):   greed

plough (n.):   a tool used for lifting and turning over soil

consolation (n.): the act of comforting someone

Introduce **Reproducible 10B1: "The Fox and the Horse."**

- What is the conflict in this story? How does the horse feel when this happens?
- What does the fox notice when he sees the horse? What does he ask the horse next?
- How does the fox help the horse? Why do you think he decides to do this?
- How does this act of kindness save the horse? What would the horse's life have been like if the fox hadn't helped him? How did teamwork lead to a happy ending in this story?
- What quality did the horse need to possess in order to allow the fox to help him?
- What is the theme or message of this story? Write it in the form of a sentence. How do you know? Use two examples from the text to support your answer.
- Reflection question: How can teamwork help us to overcome obstacles and solve problems in our lives?

Distribute **Reproducible 10B2: Understanding Plot in a Fable**. Carry out the instructions in it.

ACTIVITY 10C Preserving Friendship

ELA Goal: Students will analyze how the poet's use of imagery contributes to the overall meaning of the poem. Students will identify and explain the speaker's tone in the poem.

SEL Goal—Social Awareness: Students will practice perspective-taking, role playing, and discuss conflict resolution through poetry analysis. Students will understand the importance of reflection and communication in relationship building.

Materials Needed: Journal or notebook, **Reproducible 10C1: "Preserving Friendship," Reproducible 10C2: Words to Describe Different Tones in Literature**.

"Preserving Friendship"

We Have Been Friends Together By Caroline Norton	

We have been friends together,
   In sunshine and in shade;
Since first beneath the chestnut-trees
   In infancy we played.
But coldness dwells within thy heart,
   A cloud is on thy brow;
We have been friends together—
   Shall a light word part us now?
 	
We have been gay together;
   We have laugh'd at little jests;
For the fount of hope was gushing
   Warm and joyous in our breasts.
But laughter now hath fled thy lip,
   And sullen glooms thy brow;
We have been gay together—
   Shall a light word part us now?
 	
We have been sad together,
   We have wept, with bitter tears,
O'er the grass-grown graves, where slumber'd
   The hopes of early years.
The voices which are silent there
   Would bid thee clear thy brow;
We have been sad together—
   Oh! what shall part us now?	

Words to Describe Different Tones in Literature

Positive	Neutral	Negative
appreciative	curious	anxious
hopeful	questioning	confused
excited	reflective	mournful
friendly	direct	conflicted
encouraging	indirect	angry
reflective		disappointed
confident		fearful
romantic		melancholy
playful		uncertain
proud		doubtful

Journal Prompt: Describe a time when you have experienced a conflict with a friend. What happened? What do you think caused it? How did you feel? How do you think the other person felt? Did you ever reach a resolution? If so, what was it? If not, why?

Pass out **Reproducible 10C1: "Preserving Friendship."**

PRE-READING Vocabulary

thy (pronoun):   your

thee (pronoun):   you

gay (adj.):   happy

jests (n.):   jokes

fount (n.):   fountain

sullen (adj.):   sad

slumber'd (v.):   slept

PART 1 Directions

As you read the poem, pause after each stanza and summarize each section in your own words.

Paraphrase/Text-to-Self Connection Practice: I Remember/Say Something

Students read silently a designated section of lines from the poem (we recommend pausing every four lines). At the determined break, the first student says " 'I Remember' the author said . . ." or as an example, "I Remember the two friends used to spend a lot of time together. . . ." The second student responds to what the first student remembered, offering an elaboration, reaction, or reflection on the line shared. "I Remember/Say Something" gets students talking about text through responses/reactions to what their partner student noticed.

Exercise on author's tone: What is tone? There should be a more apparent break here between this activity and the previous one.

- The speaker's attitude in a work of literature. For example:

Your mother says "Don't use that tone with me!" In other words, "Don't speak to me with a rude attitude!"

Authors can write using different tones in their texts, just as people can speak in different tones with their voices.

What is the author's tone in this poem? Use three examples from the text to support your answer.

ACTIVITY 10D "We Have Been Friends Together" Writing Activities

PART 2 Directions

ELA Goal: Students will write a letter in which they evaluate the conflict in the poem and analyze ways in which one could reach a resolution.

Students will use examples from the poem to support their proposed solution to the speaker's conflict.

SEL Goal—Social Awareness: Students will practice perspective-taking, role playing, and conflict resolution through creative writing.

Relationship Skills: Students will practice identifying, evaluating, and solving conflicts through communication in relationship building.

Materials Needed: Journal or notebook.

Revisit student journal prompt in which they reflected upon a time when they experienced a conflict with a friend. Write a 10-line "Poem for Two Voices," exploring the two different perspectives involved in the incident—their own as well as their friend's.

Note: There are several examples of "Poems for Two Voices" easily located on the internet. An excellent print resource is *Joyful Noise: Poems for Two Voices* by Paul Fleischman.

Notes

1 Maslow, 1998.
2 Weng & others, 2013.
3 Galinksy, 2010, p. 71.
4 Grimm & Grimm, 1815.

11

Demonstrate Leadership

Effective leaders:

- Want their people to succeed.
- Are not competitive with their team.
- Have an open-door policy (are generous with their time).
- Would rather err on the side of grace than be just or strict with policies.
- Are open to new ideas.
- Freely share what they are learning.
- Love to give credit to others even when they could rightly keep it for themselves.
- Care about their team. They know about each team member's goals and dreams, and diligently try to help them fulfill those desires.[1]

All of these qualities of a successful leader are included in the five traits that CASEL identifies as to an individual's success in life (see Chapter 1). These qualities bring success in life, not only for those students that are in leadership positions but for all students. If you can imagine your students having all or some of these traits, you would see a classroom where high levels of learning take place. Management consultant Sharon Salzberg posits that success in the workplace is most likely when eight pillars are in place. These pillars are also important for children:

- *Balance*: the ability to differentiate between who you are and what your job is.

- *Concentration*: the ability to focus without being swayed by distraction.
- *Compassion*: being aware of and sympathetic to the humanity of others.
- *Resilience*: the ability to recover from defeat, frustration, or failure.
- *Communication and connection*: understanding that everything we do and say can improve connection or take away from it.
- *Integrity*: integrating your deepest ethical values into all you do.
- *Meaning*: infusing the work you do with relevance for your own personal goals.
- *Open awareness*: the ability to see the big picture and not be held back by self-imposed limitations.[2]

Students' daily lives involve "work," and their "jobs" entail these precise skills. As we grow throughout our lifetimes, the setting may change, but the fundamental skills that help us succeed remain constant. Authentic leadership requires the "bandwidth" and flexibility to help guide a group or organization. One element that has been acknowledged recently in the media is "focus." Famed emotional intelligence researcher Daniel Goleman states:

Leadership itself hinges on effectively capturing and directing the collective attention.

Leading attention requires these elements: focusing your own attention, then attracting and directing attention from others, and getting and keeping the attention of employees and peers, of customers and clients.[3]

Popular media and characters from literature dating back to the Old Testament portray leaders as being in positions of power. The situations in which these traditional examples of leaders find themselves often include conflict, such as battles and struggles for control over people and possessions. Providing insight into power, Congressman Tim Ryan notes that our perceptions have been influenced over thousands of years by

millennia of warrior traditions . . . focused on training two qualities: wisdom and bravery. Wisdom is defined as the ability to see clearly how things are, not how we want them to be, and then use that information to make the most effective decision in the moment. Bravery . . . is the ability to stay present with any experience, even an extremely difficult one, without needing it to be different.[4]

Previously essential? Probably. Essential today? Probably not.

As children develop skills and strategies tied to decision-making—big and small—they learn to make choices about what to ignore and where to focus their attention. This awareness brings with it a responsibility to balance difficult, sometimes contrary elements in order to achieve a desired outcome. Congressman Ryan refers to this as

> the ability to be firm and simultaneously to be gentle. This can be challenging, but Martin Luther King, Jr. offered us an example of holding hard and soft together. He pointed out that love without power is ineffectual, and power without love is destructive.[5]

Leadership entails skill in handling and distributing power and making calculated choices. Also implicit in the notion of leadership is the understanding that others choose to follow the inspiration of a leader.

> Leaders who inspire can articulate shared values that resonate with and motivate the group. These are the leaders people love to work with, who surface the vision that moves everyone. But to speak from the heart, to the heart, a leader must first know her values. That takes self-awareness.[6]

Self-awareness, a vital aspect of leadership, includes having an accurate image of one's strengths and weaknesses. This affords children the opportunity to view themselves as protagonists, directors, and authors of their own stories. Leaders who have a strong awareness of themselves are better able to gain the trust of others. Former president of Wellesley College Diana Walsh stated "Trustworthy leaders are poets; they quarrel with themselves."[7]

As children become more self-aware, they naturally realize that the self is part of a bigger system. They recognize that we are not alone, and that the goal is not independence from family and friends. Rather, it is interdependence with them. This often stirs questions about doing something for one's self in a selfish manner, and doing something for one's self as part of important self-care. Ultimately, children will come to understand that when we "water the seeds of peace in ourselves and those around us, we become alive, and we can help ourselves and others realize peace and compassion."[8] This is among the best goals of leadership.

As Goleman puts it, "[the] most visible leadership abilities build not just on empathy, but also on managing ourselves and sensing how what we do affects others."[9] Demonstrating leadership is one way that children portray their social-emotional competence. The following activities are designed to improve this competence by having children understand power and by expanding their capacity for self-awareness.

ACTIVITY 11A What Makes a Good Leader?

ELA Goal—Literacy: Conduct research investigating a well-known figure of leadership. Answer questions that drawn on the SEL tenets of leadership and relate back to the essential questions of the unit. Present findings to the class and initiate a discussion on the topic of leadership.

SEL Goal—Social Awareness: Recognize qualities that are associated with people who have demonstrated successful leadership.

Relationship Skills: Examine examples of individuals who have employed clear inspiring and empowering communication, have worked cooperatively by building relationships with others, and have worked actively to improve society and resolve conflicts.

Self-Management: Analyze figures who have demonstrated self-motivation and have set and achieved goals.

Responsible Decision-Making: Investigate models of ethical and responsible actions.

Materials Needed: A box or receptacle for use in conducting research topic lottery, **Reproducible 11A1: Anticipation Guide, Reproducible 11A2: Research Findings**, internet access for research.

Anticipation Guide

- What makes a good leader?
- What characteristics does a good leader possess?
- How do leaders inspire and empower others?
- What is the difference between leadership and power?

Research Findings

Students are to answer the following questions in their research (ideas for questions):

1. Summarize this person's life story (e.g., where and when this person lived, what he or she did to create change, what he or she is known for).
2. What contribution did this person make in history?
3. How did he or she accomplish this?
4. Why did he or she accomplish this?
5. How did his or her actions impact the world?
6. What do you find interesting about this person? Why?
7. What questions would you ask this person? Why?

Critical thinking:

1. What experiences did this person have that motivated him or her to make change?
2. What was his or her goal? Did he or she accomplish it?
3. How did this person inspire and empower others?
4. What leadership characteristics did this person possess? Support with examples from your research.

Possible Implementations of **Reproducible 11A1: Anticipation Guide**:

- Write responses on the board or on chart paper.
- Students write their responses on chart paper and present to the class after an allotted amount of time.
- Students respond to questions on sticky notes and stick responses to charts.
- Students respond on their devices using Mentimeter, using each question on **Reproducible 11A1: Anticipation Guide** as an open-ended question. Students project responses on board.

Explain that the class is going to study well-known leaders from history and then return to the questions at the conclusion of the project to see how their answers may have changed.

Prior to the lesson, write the names of well-known leaders on index cards to create a "lottery" from which students will choose their research topic. Place the cards in a box or receptacle so students can pick their leader.

Hand out **Reproducible 11A2: Research Findings** with guidelines for research project.

Students are to find at least three (more or less, whatever you deem appropriate) websites with information on student's research topic.

Students will answer research questions from **Reproducible 11A2: Research Findings** and present their findings to their peers (small groups or whole-class presentation).

Students may use their chosen medium to present their information: PowerPoint, Prezi, Glogster, original video, children's book, narrative or lyric poem, poster board, or song.

OPTIONAL

Students complete a Research Self-Assessment reflecting on their process in conducting and organizing research, overcoming challenges, and meeting guideline requirements.

ACTIVITY 11B Inspiring and Empowering Through Language

AL Goal—Literacy: Identify purpose and central message in a famous speech; analyze figurative and connotative language as well as structure used to communicate this message.

SEL Goal—Responsible Decision-Making: Help students recognize the power of words and the role of language in inspiring and empowering others.

Materials Needed: **Reproducible 11B1Nelson Mandela's Inaugural Speech From 1994, Reproducible 11B2: Station Rotation Questions**, desks set up as rotation stations, student devices.

Additional Materials: While this lessons focuses on two speeches specifically, this lesson can be used with several famous speeches, such as Martin Luther King Jr.'s "I Have a Dream" speech, Abraham Lincoln's Gettysburg Address, Patrick Henry's "Speech at the Virginia Convention," Barack Obama's 2009 Inaugural Address, and many others. For a helpful site that provides several speeches for middle level readers, refer to www.mocomi.com.

Prior to the lesson, separate students into groups of three or four.

Nelson Mandela's Inaugural Speech From 1994

1. What is this speaker's position (job) and background?
2. Where was this speech delivered?
3. What important historical events happened at the time that this speech was delivered?
4. Who is this speaker's audience?

STATEMENT OF THE PRESIDENT OF THE AFRICAN NATIONAL CONGRESS, NELSON MANDELA, AT HIS INAUGURATION AS PRESIDENT OF THE DEMOCRATIC REPUBLIC OF SOUTH AFRICA, UNION BUILDINGS, PRETORIA, MAY 10, 1994

Your Majesties, Your Highnesses, Distinguished Guests, Comrades, and Friends:

Today, all of us do, by our presence here, and by our celebrations in other parts of our country and the world, confer glory and hope to newborn liberty.

Out of the experience of an extraordinary human disaster that lasted too long, must be born a society of which all humanity will be proud.

Our daily deeds as ordinary South Africans must produce an actual South African reality that will reinforce humanity's belief in justice, strengthen its confidence in the nobility of the human soul and sustain all our hopes for a glorious life for all.

All this we owe both to ourselves and to the peoples of the world who are so well represented here today.

To my compatriots, I have no hesitation in saying that each one of us is as intimately attached to the soil of this beautiful country as are the famous jacaranda trees of Pretoria and the mimosa trees of the bushveld.

Each time one of us touches the soil of this land, we feel a sense of personal renewal. The national mood changes as the seasons change.

We are moved by a sense of joy and exhilaration when the grass turns green and the flowers bloom.

That spiritual and physical oneness we all share with this common homeland explains the depth of the pain we all carried in our hearts as we saw our country tear itself apart in a terrible conflict, and as we saw it spurned, outlawed, and isolated by the peoples of the world, precisely because it has become the universal base of the pernicious ideology and practice of racism and racial oppression.

We, the people of South Africa, feel fulfilled that humanity has taken us back into its bosom, that we, who were outlaws not so long ago, have today been given the rare privilege to be host to the nations of the world on our own soil.

We thank all our distinguished international guests for having come to take possession with the people of our country of what is, after all, a common victory for justice, for peace, for human dignity.

We trust that you will continue to stand by us as we tackle the challenges of building peace, prosperity, non-sexism, non-racialism and democracy.

We deeply appreciate the role that the masses of our people and their political mass democratic, religious, women, youth, business, traditional, and other leaders have played to bring about this conclusion. Not least among them is my Second Deputy President, the Honorable F. W. de Klerk.

We would also like to pay tribute to our security forces, in all their ranks, for the distinguished role they have played in securing our first democratic elections and the transition to democracy, from blood-thirsty forces which still refuse to see the light.

The time for the healing of the wounds has come.

The moment to bridge the chasms that divide us has come.

The time to build is upon us.

We have, at last, achieved our political emancipation. We pledge ourselves to liberate all our people from the continuing bondage of poverty, deprivation, suffering, gender, and other discrimination.

We succeeded to take our last steps to freedom in conditions of relative peace. We commit ourselves to the construction of a complete, just, and lasting peace.

We have triumphed in the effort to implant hope in the breasts of the millions of our people. We enter into a covenant that we shall build the society in which all South Africans, both black and white, will be able to walk tall, without any fear in their hearts, assured of their inalienable right to human dignity—a rainbow nation at peace with itself and the world.

As a token of its commitment to the renewal of our country, the new Interim Government of National Unity will, as a matter of urgency, address the issue of amnesty for various categories of our people who are currently serving terms of imprisonment.

We dedicate this day to all the heroes and heroines in this country and the rest of the world who sacrificed in many ways and surrendered their lives so that we could be free.

Their dreams have become reality. Freedom is their reward.

We are both humbled and elevated by the honor and privilege that you, the people of South Africa, have bestowed on us, as the first President of a united, democratic, non-racial and non-sexist South Africa, to lead our country out of the valley of darkness.

We understand it still that there is no easy road to freedom.

We know it well that none of us acting alone can achieve success.

We must therefore act together as a united people, for national reconciliation, for nation building, for the birth of a new world.

Let there be justice for all.

Let there be peace for all.

Let there be work, bread, water, and salt for all.

Let each know that for each the body, the mind and the soul have been freed to fulfill themselves.

Never, never, and never again shall it be that this beautiful land will again experience the oppression of one by another and suffer the indignity of being the skunk of the world.

Let freedom reign.

The sun shall never set on so glorious a human achievement!

God bless Africa!

Thank you.

Station Rotation Questions

Station #1: Diction and Tone

1. Highlight the most important words and phrases in this speech. Notice what stands out to you. Why do you think these words and phrases stand out to you?
2. Are there any words that are repeated? Which ones?
3. Notice the general feeling that you get from these words. Do they seem like words with positive or negative meanings? Why?
4. What kind of attitude does the speaker seem to have? What is his/her tone?
5. Notice the pronouns (e.g., he, she, me, I, we, us, them, they) the speaker uses. Underline the pronouns. What pronouns are used most often? Why?

Station #2: Persuasive Devices

1. What persuasive devices does the speaker use in this speech? Refer to the following list:
   - Ethos (describing his/her experience, authority, credibility)
   - Pathos (appealing to the audience's emotions, trying to make them feel a specific way through emotive language or stories)
   - Logos (using facts, logic, or reason)
   - Compare/contrast
   - Cause/effect
2. Write at least three examples in your chart.
3. How do you think these devices help the speaker to persuade the audience/communicate the message?

Station #3: Literary Devices

1. What literary devices does the speaker use in this speech? Refer to the following list:
   - imagery
   - personification
   - metaphor
   - extended metaphor
   - simile
   - sensory details
   - onomatopoeia
   - alliteration
   - allusion
   - parallel structure
   - rhythm/rhyme
2. Write at least three examples in your chart.
3. How do you think these devices help the speaker to communicate the message?

Station #4: Theme/Message/Reader Response

1. What do you think is the theme/message of this speech? What is the point that the speaker is trying to get across?
2. Now imagine yourself as a member of this speaker's audience. How does this speech make you feel? Inspired? Empowered? Hopeful? Optimistic? Reflective? Why?
3. What is your favorite sentence or passage from this speech? Why?
4. What questions do you have for this speaker/about this speech?

For homework the night before, as part of a blended learning playlist, or as a warm-up for the lesson, have students use their devices to complete a webquest that addresses questions at the beginning of **Reproducible 11B1: Nelson Mandela's Inaugural Speech From 1994**.

Next, have students read the speech as a class, individually, or in pairs.

Then, students are to get into their station groups and answer the questions at each station to further analyze the speech with **Reproducible 11B2: Station Rotation Questions**.

Note: This activity can be repeated with a second or third speech example for a compare/contrast activity. Ask students to notice similarities and differences, comparing use of persuasive and literary devices, message, tone, and purpose.

ACTIVITY 11C Poetry Analysis Shields

AL Goal: Analyze imagery, theme, and tone in poetry.

SEL Goal—Self-Awareness: Help students identify their own strengths and connection to others.

Materials Needed: **Reproducible 11C1: Personal Shield, Reproducible 11C2: Sonnet Guiding Questions**, crayons, markers, colored pencils.

Personal Shield

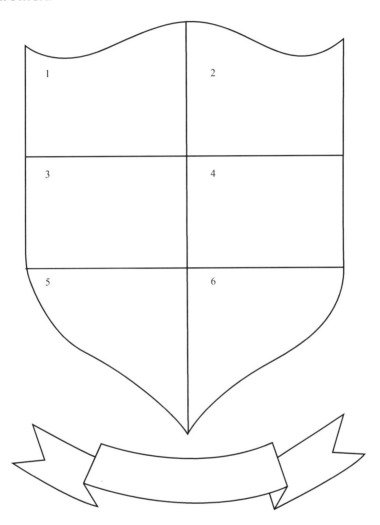

Read the sonnet located here: www.poetryfoundation.org/poems/49052/sonnet-56d22aca442e3.

Then answer the Guiding Questions on the next handout.

Sonnet Guiding Questions

Guided Reading Questions:

1. Diction: circle the words that stand out to you in this poem.
2. Highlight or underline examples of imagery in this poem.
3. What do you think is the poet's message? Why? Explain how the word that you have circled and the examples of imagery you have found support this message.
4. How would you describe the tone of this poem? What is his attitude? What words give you this impression?

Art Activity:

1. Now imagine that you are about to face an obstacle in which you will need to show courage. Complete the shield graphic organizer by illustrating the images that the poet uses to communicate his message.
2. Refer back to your journal prompt response. Now, think about the obstacle that was the focus of your writing. If you could create your own shield for yourself, what symbolic images would you use to arm yourself in your own "battle"?
3. Illustrate a shield for yourself, using your own symbolic images.
4. In small groups, explain why you chose these symbolic images and what they mean to you. How could this "shield" help you to face your own battles?

Journal Prompt: Describe a time in which you have faced a great challenge. What was it? How did you face this challenge?

REPRODUCIBLE 11C: Personal Shield Questions
PRE-READING Vocabulary

falter (v.):   to attempt something with little confidence

utter (v.):   to speak

raven (n.):   a large crow with shiny black feathers

hindering (adj.):   difficult; hiding

shrouds (n.):   coverings as in a large piece of cloth

Distribute **Reproducible 11C1: Personal Shield, Reproducible 11C2: Sonnet Guiding Questions**, crayons, markers, colored pencils.

ACTIVITY 11D Interviewing Our Leaders

AL Goal—Literacy: Conduct research through an interview and organize relevant information into a concise and coherent presentation.

SEL Goal—Relationships: Students will recognize a figure of leadership in their lives, and practice communication skills in a one-on-one setting.

Materials Needed: **Reproducible 11D1: "Interviewing Our Leaders."**

"Interviewing Our Leaders"

Guiding Questions for Interview:

1. Growing up, who was your role model? Why?
2. How would you define a good leader?
3. How do you think you have been able to make an impact in today's world?
4. What motivates/inspires/empowers you?
5. What changes would you like to make in our world?
6. What makes you want to make this change?
7. What has been your proudest moment? Why?
8. What has been your biggest challenge? How did you cope with it?
9. What would you like to be your legacy?
10. What advice would you give to future leaders?

After the interview, students should answer the following questions:

1. Why did you choose this person as a leader in your life?
2. How would you describe this person?
3. During the interview, what did you learn? What surprised you? What did you find interesting?
4. Is there anything about this person you would like to emulate? If so, what? Why?

A good follow-up activity to the mini-research project on a famous leader is an interview between your students and a role model whom they consider to be a good leader in their own lives. He or she could be a parent, grandparent, aunt, uncle, sibling, cousin, coach, teacher, religious leader, scout leader, administrator, local politician, or other community member. Similar to the research project, students can compile their research through an interview and present it in the form of a written response after using **Reproducible 11D1: "Interviewing Our Leaders."**

Ideas for a written assessment include:

- A journalistic feature story
- Narrative reflective essay
- Prezi, Glogster, or PowerPoint

Students can present their results to small groups or the whole class. Distribute **Reproducible 11D1: "Interviewing Our Leaders."**

Notes

1 Stevens, 2015, p. 1.
2 Salzberg, 2013, p. 5.
3 Goleman & others, 2013, p. 210.
4 Ryan, 2012, p. 116.
5 Ryan, 2012, p. 169.
6 Goleman & others, 2013, p. 225.
7 Walsh, 2006.
8 Nhat Hanh, 2008, p. 12.
9 Goleman & others, 2013, p. 235.

Part V
Responsible Decision-Making

12

Think Creatively

To be considered creative, must a person's achievements bring widespread recognition? We do not think so. As Shank and Cleary point out, simply getting through a typical day in the modern world requires imagination. "These small acts of creativity, though they differ in scope, are not different in kind from the brilliant leaps of an Einstein. Creativity is a commonplace in cognition, not an esoteric gift bequeathed only to a few."[1]

So what do we know about ordinary creativity? First of all, it is not now and probably never was equally distributed over time. As Zhoa reports:

> There were less than 10 major inventions between 1 AD and 1800 AD. Contrast that to the last 200 years, during which time we have seen the creation of more than 25 life-altering technological and social inventions, such as computers, antibiotics, airplanes, internet, genetic engineering, organ transplants, automobiles, lasers, and telecommunication. Consider this: if you had been born more than 2,000 years ago it would have been possible to live your entire life without being impacted by a life-changing invention. When you live in the 21st century, a time fraught with change, that's pretty hard to imagine.[2]

At the present time, education in Western societies has swung toward content knowledge (academic curriculum—AL), as measured by standardized tests. In Eastern societies, where content knowledge was prominent for centuries, a more equitable balance between SEL and academic goals is being sought. For example, as recent research has found,

> Chinese student scores on an annual international assessment of creativity have been rapidly rising since 1990, whereas American scores have been decreasing. The test is considered valid by scholars, and has a high correlation with success later in life.[3]

There is an underlying assumption about creativity implicit in these statements: *creativity can be learned*. As we said in Chapter 1, it helps to have good genes. Nevertheless, social and emotional factors, including education, can raise a learner's potential greatly. Let's see some examples.

ACTIVITY 12A. What's in the Box?

AL Goal—Literacy: Describe in depth a character, setting, or event in a story or drama, drawing on specific details in the text (e.g., a character's thoughts, words, or actions).

SEL Goal—Responsible Decision-Making: Choosing the right character, setting, or event to create a high-quality story in a limited amount of time.

Materials Needed: Paper and pencil, **Reproducible 12A1: Maxie, the Chipmunk**.

Maxie, the Chipmunk

Tell your students to write a story about the scene in **Reproducible 12A1: Maxie, the Chipmunk**. There is no right way to write it. Be as imaginative as you can! (Allow 10 minutes.)

You might want to mention the following study to the class. In their research on imaginative problem solving, John Dacey and Richard Ripple[4] evaluated the stories from 1,200 fourth- through eighth-grade students about this picture. Amazingly, about 900 of the stories were almost exactly alike! (They were about how the animal's curiosity became its undoing.) The other 300 stories, however, were decidedly different from each other. Here is one of those stories by a sixth grader:

A Tail [*sic*] about a Frighted [*sic*] Chipmunk

Chuckie the chipmunk was chasing a beetle. He was starving.

The red sky above him was dark and stormy. The leafy ground in the forest was smelly. Chuckie wondered how he was going to get any food. He thought of last night and the monsters. Some had four sharp claws, others had huge round eyes. He was so scared!

Suddenly a bear jumped out of the bushes . . . (the story ends because time ran out.)

As in this story, the students who wrote the better stories frequently used the red square in the picture merely as a departure point. From there, they could travel to other, more outlandish places. Many saw it as a window or a door through which they could leave the simple scene. Others stretched their imaginations to describe it as a time capsule, a case of TNT, a casket, the sky, or a player piano. A small number disregarded the square altogether.

Ask students to answer two simple questions:

1. "Honestly, was your story more like the 900 ordinary ones, or the 300 extraordinary ones?"
2. "Knowing what you know now, would you like to try again?"

ACTIVITY 12B What Do You Notice? What Do You Wonder?

ELA Goal: Reasoning about shapes and their attributes, and explaining in technical language how to describe what happens when shapes are changed.

SEL Goal—Relationship Skills: Improve interpersonal problem-solving skills.

Materials Needed: Paper and pencil, **Reproducible 12B1: Circles Within Circles**.

This activity would work well as an interdisciplinary/co-teaching lesson with a mathematics teacher.

Circles Within Circles

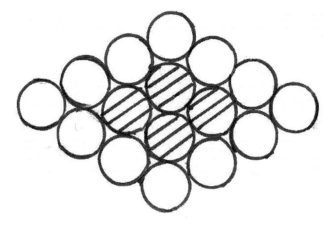

Two More Circles Within Circles

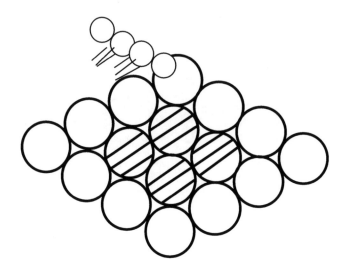

Show students **Reproducible 12B1**: **Circles Within Circles.** In this activity, they should try to notice all the aspects of a geometric figure. Examples of what they might come up with are:

- The outside shape is a diamond.
- The inside shape is a diamond.
- There are four shaded circles.
- There are 12 open circles.
- You can see a lot of triangles within this picture.
- What are the relationships between a diamond and a parallelogram?

To promote this type of imaginative thinking, the National Council of Teachers of Mathematics suggests that you "create a safe environment where students focus on sharing their thoughts without any pressure to solve a problem."[5]

Now you want them to wonder. Ask them to think what would happen if two more shaded circles were added inside to blank circles. Show them **Reproducible 12B2: Two More Circles Within Circles B** Ask how many blank circles you need to add to enclose the shaded circles again? (The answer is two.)

Now ask about adding 38 shaded circles: how many open circles do you need to add to enclose the shaded circles again? Many students will try to figure this out by actually drawing the circles. (The answer is 38; you always need to add the same number of open circles as the number of shaded circles you have added.) Ask them if they notice a relationship between the number of shaded circles and open circles. Can they think of a simple formula for answering this question? Ask if they can think of any other questions. (One might be what happens to the diamond shape when you add shaded circles? The shape becomes a parallelogram.)

ACTIVITY 12C Litter-ally

ELA Goal: Collect data scientifically, graph it, and write a cogent report to be presented to town officials using clear and concise language that is relevant to task and audience.

SEL Goal—Social Awareness: Using imagination to better understand human behavior.

Materials Needed: Paper and pencil; 10 pieces of string, each 1 yard long; large garbage bags, one for every three children in your class; **Reproducible 12C1: Types of Litter**.

Types of Litter

TYPES OF LITTER	CHILDREN	TEENAGERS	ADULTS	ANYONE
Bottles				
Cans				
Plastic bags				
School papers				
Candy wrappers				
Other food wrappers				
Other items—list here:				
Totals:				

The purpose of this activity is to help students assess the litter problem around their school, and if you choose, other areas in the neighborhood. They will use creative thinking to solve a problem by inferring who is responsible for the litter. By noting the number of hours the students have devoted to this process, the cost to the town (if town workers have been employed) can also be calculated.

Explain to the students that you are going to show them how to collect data about litter around their school. They are going to categorize the data, graph it, and make a report to the Department of Public Works in hopes of reducing the unsightly problem.

Show them **Reproducible 12C1: Types of Litter**. This will be the form they will use to collect their data for the report. You might begin this research by discussing of the meaning of the word "litter." When the students have agreed on a definition, tell them to use the following steps to collect the data:

1. Have them count off by threes.
2. The groups are to go into the schoolyard and find different areas of litter.
3. One student in each group should hold out her arms to define the collection area. It should not overlap with anyone else's collection area.
4. Use one piece of string to define a circle on the ground around her feet approximately one yard in diameter.
5. Using one of the garbage bags, collect all the litter in that circle.

Bring the litter inside and categorize it, using **Reproducible 12C1: Types of Litter**. At least two of the students must agree on the category of each item. Combine all of the small group reports into one master report and a copy of **Reproducible 12C1**. When the master data sheet is completed, explain to the students how to graph the data.

Now they need to work together to prepare a document on their findings to the Department of Public Works. An important part of this report will be their determination of which age group is mainly responsible for the litter. They should brainstorm ideas that need to go into the report and then elect a committee of five students to prepare it. It should be sent to the superintendent of the department, and then a meeting with her should be arranged. Finally, this committee should report back to the class on what actions the superintendent said would be taken.

ACTIVITY 12D Creatively Matching Ideas

ELA Goal: Using word association to better understand vocabulary.

SEL Goal—Self-Awareness: Becoming more aware of one's creative abilities through a cognitive challenge.

Materials Needed: Paper and pencil, **Reproducible 12D1: Pairing Challenge, Reproducible 12D2: Answers to the Pairing Challenge**.

Pairing Challenge

In this exercise, you are presented with three words and asked to find a fourth word which is related to those three. Note: the first three words have little to do with each other, but all three *are* associated with the fourth word. That is the one you are to guess. For example, what word do you think is related to these three?

cookies sugar heart _____

The answer in this case is "sweet." Cookies are sweet; so is sugar, and sweet is part of the word "sweetheart."

Here is another example: fast go molasses _____

You should have written the word "slow" in the answer space, because it goes with each of the other words. "Slow" is the opposite of "fast," it's part of the phrase "go slow," and also a part of the phrase "slow as molasses." As you can see, the fourth word can be related to the other three for different reasons. You really have to use your imagination!

Now try these sets of three words. Write the word you think is correct in the space following the three words. Don't spend too much time trying to get any one answer. You have 7 minutes.

1. Jill	tire	beanstalk	_____
2. mountain	low	skyscraper	_____
3. package	cardboard	ring	_____
4. surprise	presents	birthday	_____
5. crazy	salted	pecan	_____
6. connect	high	electric	_____
7. butterfly	catch	fish	_____
8. sun	bulb	heavy	_____
9. slit	knife	Band-Aid	_____
10. snow	color	black	_____
11. building	house	plate	_____
12. slugger	wood	ball	_____
13. stage	game	actor	_____
14. Roman	arithmetic	VII	_____
15. cat	white	dark	_____
16. round	bat	beach	_____

Answers to the Pairing Challenge

1. jack

2. high

3. box

4. party

5. nut

6. wire

7. net

8. light

9. cut

10. white

11. home

12. bat

13. play

14. numeral

15. black

16. ball

Present **Reproducible 12D1: Pairing Challenge**. After 7 minutes, ask students to swap answers with another pupil, then read the answers. Tell them you will bet that for any one item, at least one student will have gotten the right answer. After scoring, ask if anyone got them all right.

Pass out or read from the answer sheet, **Reproducible 12D2: Answers to the Pairing Challenge**. Explain that creativity is the process by which ideas already in the mind are paired in unusual and useful combinations. Every image or concept we have is associated with other images and concepts. When people think about solving a problem, they mentally cast about for an association that might serve as a solution. Most of us accept the first idea that seems to solve the problem. Creative people are those who go further down the mental list, searching for more unusual but higher quality pairings to solve their problems. It is these remote pairings that produce creative ideas.

Now ask students to discuss the following questions:

- Do you believe this is a fair test of creativity?
- Do you think your score represents your actual ability?
- What are some reasons we might want to measure creative ability with a simple test like this?

ACTIVITY 12E Lateral Thinking

ELA Goal: Understand and invent sayings (adages, maxims, proverbs) in imaginative, unique ways.

SEL Goal—Social Awareness: What common sayings indicate about us as human beings.

Materials Needed: Paper and pencil, **Reproducible 12E1: Common Sayings (Animals), Reproducible 12E2: Some Other Common Sayings**.

Common Sayings (Animals)

1. A _____ in the hand is worth two in the bush.
2. When the cat's away the _____ will play.
3. Don't count your _____ before they are hatched.
4. Like water off a _____ back.
5. You can catch more _____ with honey than you can with vinegar.
6. There are plenty of _____ in the sea.

(Teacher: Answers to **Reproducible 12E1: Common Sayings (Animals)**: bird; mice; chickens; duck's; flies; fish.)

Some Other Common Sayings

A fool and her money are soon parted.
It takes one to know one.
Better late than never.
An apple doesn't fall far from the tree.

Lateral thinking is typical "outside the box" creative thinking used when a straight-ahead, linear, step-by-step approach may not be as productive. Tell students the game they are going to play promotes something called "lateral thinking." It uses such common sayings as, "You can get more bees with honey than with vinegar." Here are some others they might try: **Reproducible 12E1: Common Sayings (Animals)**.

As another example, pass out **Reproducible 12E2: Some Other Common Sayings**. Think of as many of these adages as possible, and write down the first part of each one on an index card. For example, you would write "The apple doesn't fall . . ." or "It takes one to. . . ." The point of this game is to come up with funny endings.

Put all your cards in a brown paper bag. Each player chooses a card from the bag and then has 15 seconds to come up with a different, funny ending for the saying. For example, if you pick "The apple doesn't fall . . .," you might come up with the ending "if you're holding onto it really tight."

After all the cards are used, discuss which of the endings each of you found the funniest. Answer the question: "What has this got to do with creativity?"

THIS JUST IN! (from the *New York Times*)[6]

> Small rocks from the beaches of eastern Massachusetts began appearing at Lexington High School last fall. They were painted in pastels and inscribed with pithy advice: *Be happy. . . . Mistakes are O.K. . . . Don't worry, it will be over soon.* They had appeared almost by magic, boosting spirits and spreading calm at a public high school known for its sleep-deprived student body.
>
> Crying jags over test scores are common here. Students say getting B's can be deeply dispiriting, dashing college dreams and profoundly disappointing parents.
>
> The rocks, it turns out, were the work of a small group of students worried about rising anxiety and depression among their peers. They had transformed a storage area into a relaxation center with comfy chairs, an orange/peach lava lamp and a coffee table brimming with donated art supplies and lots and lots of rocks—to be painted and given to favorite teachers and friends. They call it the Rock Room.

Now, that's SEL! So, you have some models to follow. We hope you will spend a lot of time nurturing your students' creativity. Our planet needs you to do so—desperately!

Notes

1 Schank & Cleary, 1995, p. 229.
2 Zhao, 2014, p. 1.
3 "The Creativity Crisis," July 2010.
4 Dacey & Ripple, 1969.
5 NCTM, 2016, p. 1.
6 Spencer, April 5, 2017.

13

Think Critically and Wisely

What is critical thinking, exactly? Critical thinking is the intellectually disciplined process of actively and skillfully conceptualizing, applying, analyzing, synthesizing, and/or evaluating information gathered from, or generated by, observation, experience, reflection, reasoning, or communication, as a guide to belief and action.[1] Whew. That's a mouthful! Here's another definition: *the awakening of the intellect to the study of itself.*[2] That, we think, is the heart of critical thinking. It differs from independent thinking in that it relies more on logic and less on social relations.

The opposite of critical thinking is murky and irrational thought. Current educational practices in too many classrooms around the planet tend to promote cautious, compliant memorization as opposed to bold reflection. This leaves many students feeling fuzzy-headed and uninspired. When children enhance their social and emotional skills, their interest in academic skills improves as well.[3] In simple terms, critical thinking examines assumptions and biases (why?), discerns hidden values and evaluates evidence (what?), and assesses conclusions (how?).[4] Educator Ian Gilbert offers a simple recommendation: "Open minds to question, to reflect, to look beneath the surface, to have beliefs that they will fight for and fight for the beliefs of others, even if they don't agree with them."[5]

ACTIVITY 13A Improving Emotional Vocabulary

ELA Goal: Expand upon students' emotional vocabulary; improve analytical skills related to character analysis; further develop a range of words that students can use to describe mood in a given setting; evaluate how writers use color to portray certain emotions.

SEL Goal: Increase self-awareness by identifying the range of words one can use to describe emotions; develop social awareness by discussing the range of emotions that others may experience, and describe facial expressions and body language that accompany various emotions.

Materials Needed: Chart paper, markers, a projector (if available), sheets of computer paper (two pieces for each student), access to a thesaurus (one per group or one per student if available), coloring supplies.

During my teaching career, I have noticed that most students tend to possess a limited vocabulary when discussing emotions. As a result, students often struggle to express themselves when they experience various emotional states. This can become problematic in any classroom, but especially one in which students are expected to comprehend, analyze, and discuss the intricate emotional workings of characters in literature. At the beginning of the year, I like to spend a class period or two discussing emotional vocabulary. This helps us when we begin to read texts and discuss character development especially. When asked to describe a character's inner worlds, students often answer with the most basic emotions: happy, sad, or mad. Using this activity will help your students think more deeply when it comes to character analysis.

1. Begin this lesson by separating the class into groups of three or four.
2. If you share a similar observation to the one I mentioned above, discuss this finding with your students. Explain to them the reasoning behind this lesson and how it will help them in the future. Begin by giving them the three basic emotion words that are often the first ones that come to mind: happy, sad, and mad. Write these on the board.
3. Instruct the students to brainstorm as many emotion words as they can with their group. Have students write their emotion words on the chart paper. Challenge them to come up with more emotions that humans can experience rather than just the three that were given to them.
4. After you have given the students enough time to brainstorm a list of emotion words, have a whole-class discussion on the words that each group came up with. Discuss any emotion words that other

students may not have thought of during this exercise. Explain how humans experience a range of emotions; our emotions exist on a spectrum. This spectrum is what they are going to create and illustrate in today's class.

5. Model an example of this for the students. Begin with the word *mad*. Show the students how one can come up with several words for this emotion that vary to a significant degree. For example, one can feel annoyed, irritated, angry, furious, incensed, enraged, or livid. Discuss how these words feel different. Is feeling annoyed the same as feeling enraged? What other words could we use to express different feelings?

6. Assign a basic emotion word to each group. For example, one group could brainstorm words for *sad*, one group or *happy*, one for *afraid*, one for *loving*, and one for *hateful* if you choose. Feel free to supplement any emotion words of your choosing. Have students use a thesaurus if necessary.

7. Give each student a piece of paper. Tell students that they are to come up with 8 to 10 emotion words for the particular emotion assigned to their group. Each student in the group must brainstorm two new words to demonstrate the range of emotions that stem from their word.

8. Once they have each come up with two new words in their group, students are to illustrate their two emotion words. Discuss the importance of color in literature, and how color can be associated with different emotions. For example, writers use the color red to symbolize danger or to foreshadow death. Writers often use red to evoke feelings of suspense and fear in the reader. Ask students to think about colors that are connected to their emotion words. This part of the activity can also be assigned for homework if necessary.

9. If there is time, or during the next class period, have the class use their emotion word illustrations to create a human spectrum. Ask students to organize themselves based on the range of emotions they created in the previous activity. Once students are standing in the order they have agreed upon, discuss why they chose to display the emotion words in this way. Ask students to think about emotions that they had not thought about before. Also, ask them why they chose particular colors for their emotion word illustrations. Suggestion: display the emotion words in the classroom and refer

back to them when discussing character development or mood in stories and poems throughout the year.

10. If there is additional time or you would like to extend this lesson, show students an illustration of this spectrum as it has been used in psychology. One suggestion is Robert Plutchik's psychoevolutionary theory of emotion, a very influential theory in this field of study. This is very easy to find and display on a projector with a brief internet search. Discuss how psychologists have also created a visual depiction of the range of human emotions just like the one students did in class. Optional: give the students a copy of this image to refer back to when writing in their journals, analyzing characters, or describing mood in literature throughout the year.

11. Extended Practice: Students think of an emotion that they learned from this activity. Choose individuals to act out this emotion and have their peers guess what word they have in mind. This can help with social awareness, as students are encouraged to consider facial expressions and body language that are recognizable when displaying certain emotions.

ACTIVITY 13B Symbolism and the Self

ELA Goal: Students will be able to identify and analyze examples of symbolism in literature.

SEL Goal—Self-Awareness: Identify and explain important aspects of one's identity; choose a symbol to represent oneself.

Materials Needed: **Reproducible 13B1: "Symbolism and the Self," Reproducible 13B1: "My Symbol, My Self."**

"Symbolism and the Self"

What is Symbolism?

A *symbol* is a thing that represents a bigger, deeper idea, feeling, or message. It is, essentially, something that you can see that stands for something you can't see.

A symbol can be:

- an object (e.g., a necklace, a lamp that is always on, a special gift)
- an animal (e.g., a singing bird, a roaring lion)
- a place (a church, the ocean, a specific restaurant where the characters always eat)
- a plant (a large pine tree that gets struck by lightning, a delicate pink rose)
- weather (a raging storm, a sunny day)

A symbol can represent:

- a theme or a message
- a mood
- a conflict that a character is experiencing
- an event that is going to happen in the future

These are just a few literary elements that can connect to a symbol . . .
Steps to Figuring Out Symbols

1. Notice when an object, an animal, a place, a plant, or weather appears over and over throughout a text.
2. Notice what is happening in the story when an image appears.
3. Notice the feeling the character has about this symbol.
4. Notice the mood of the scene when this symbol appears.
5. Notice the writer's attitude toward the symbol (e.g., respectful, sad).

If your imagination sees symbolic meaning in an object, an animal, a place, a plant, or weather—and you can justify it with evidence from story—it counts as symbolism!

Guided Practice:

Directions: Working in pairs, read the example of each type of symbol, then come up with one of your own. Be prepared to share out.

Object:
- Example 1: A lighthouse can stand for a beacon of hope in a dark time.
- Example 2:

Animal:
- Example 1: A lion often appears as a symbol of bravery in royal families.
- Example 2:

Plant:
- Example 1: A flower can stand for innocence or death.
- Example 2:

Weather:
- Example 1: A windy storm can symbolize danger ahead for the character.
- Example 2:

"My Symbol, My Self"

The symbol I have chosen to represent myself is _____.

Here is a picture of my symbol:

Literal Characteristics of My Symbol (color, texture, sound, smell, size, etc.)	Figurative Characteristics of My Symbol (e.g., what this shows about my life, why it is meaningful/special to me, how it makes me feel)
1.	
2.	
3.	
4.	
5.	

This lesson combines students' knowledge of symbolism with their self-awareness. In order for students to choose a symbol for themselves, they must have a strong understanding of symbolism prior to the second part of this lesson. Therefore, it is worth spending as much time as you feel your students need to either introduce this concept or review it with them before the second activity described here. There are several videos on the internet that can be used to introduce symbolism to students the night before as homework for this lesson. You may want to assign one of these videos for homework. Another option for reviewing symbolism with your students is to use the reproducible created below. You could use this either in addition to a video or as a stand-alone review. Using this activity along with **Reproducible 13B1: "Symbolism and the Self"** and **Reproducible 13B2: "My Symbol, My Self"** will help your students better connect with authors' use of symbolism in texts throughout the year.

PART 2

For homework, students should think of a symbol that represents something about themselves. Students should draw a picture of this symbol, and then explain its literal and figurative characteristics in the chart below. After they have explained the characteristics of their symbol, they should identify and describe what this symbol shows about them. The next day, students can explain their symbol either in pairs, small groups, or to the class. This may spark a deeper discussion on the function and role of symbolism in literature. If students start with their own self-awareness, they will be better able to analyze how writers use symbolism in texts.

ACTIVITY 13C Decisions Have Consequences

ELA Goal: Evaluate how character choices connect to the resolution of a plot; write alternate ending to a narrative.

SEL Goal—Responsible Decision-Making: Help students recognize that different decisions have different consequences.

Materials Needed: Examples from books that the students are familiar with where characters have made decisions that result in consequences. It could be a class novel or *Choose Your Own Adventure* novels, where the endings are ambiguous, cliffhangers, or otherwise undetermined.

Suggested stories for younger readers: "The Babysitter," "The Elevator," "The Guiccioli Miniature." Suggested stories for older readers: "The Most Dangerous Game," "The Scarlet Ibis," "Lamb to the Slaughter," "The Other," "The Lady or the Tiger?" **Reproducible 13C1: Decisions and Consequences**.

Decisions and Consequences

Original Decision	Consequence	Alternative Decision	Possible Consequence #1	Possible Consequence #2

JOURNAL Prompts Quick-Write

- Can you remember a time when you have made an important decision?
- What were the outcomes of your decision?
- How would things be different if you had decided differently?

1. Ask students if they've ever noticed that after making a decision, sometimes things work out fine and sometimes there are surprises. No matter how hard we might try to think of all of the risks involved in making a decision, we may forget a detail or two.
2. Describe the example from the book you have chosen and ask students to identify the decision that the character has made. Ask them to describe the outcome of the decision. Have students fill in the appropriate boxes in **Reproducible 13C1**. Ask them to think and record an alternative decision the character could have made and one or more possible consequences to that decision.
3. Have students share their alternative decisions and the possible outcomes that happened as a result. Use the following questions to lead a discussion about how decisions have consequences that we can't think of in the moment.

- Why do you think the author had the character make the choice he/she did in the story?
- What would the ideal outcome be in this story?
- What goes wrong in this story? What decision does the character make that affects the outcome of the story?
- What is the effect of this decision?
- How different were your decisions from the characters?
- How many different possible consequences did we think of?
- Why do you think this alternate decision would be appropriate for the events in this story?

EXTENDED Practice

Students should use the alternate decisions and possible consequences charts from **Reproducible 13C1: Decisions and Consequences** to write an alternate ending to the story. Students should be able to depict the character traits that they can associate with the main characters of the story and explain how the events they have altered lead to the new outcome. For an extra challenge, ask the students to write in the style of the original writer.

This will help them on standardized assessments, which often ask students to write in response to questions of this nature.

ACTIVITY 13D Reading a Photograph

ELA Goal: Make inference based on evidence in artistic text; communicate observations, connections, and inferences with well-developed, coherent explanations; collaborate with others to share inferences.

SEL Goal—Social Awareness: Practice reading facial expressions and body language; make inferences about emotions of subjects in art .

Self-Awareness: Identify emotions during self-reflection while reading works of art.

Materials Needed: Five photographs that represent the historical context of the unit, or five intriguing photographs that can be used as inspiration for a story; **Reproducible 13D1: "Reading a Photograph"; Reproducible 13D2: "Reading a Photograph" Exit Slip**; projector.

"Reading a Photograph"

People	Places
Guiding Questions: • Who is the focal point of this photograph? • What types of facial expressions do they have? • What is their body language saying? • What is the connection/relationship between the people in this photograph?	Guiding Questions: • What is the setting of this photograph? Where are they? • Is this photograph mostly light or dark? Where is the light? Where is the darkness in the photograph? • What do you notice about the landscape, weather, or conditions in the background?
Things	**Activities**
Guiding Questions: • Are there any interesting/unique objects in this photograph? What are they? • What could these objects represent? How could they be seen as symbols for something important in/about this picture?	Guiding Questions: • What are the people doing in this photograph? Why do you think they are doing this? What could be motivating them? • How do you think they are feeling while doing this activity?

"Reading a Photograph" Exit Slip

3–2–1 Inference
What are three inferences you could make based on this photograph?
What are two emotions that you feel while looking at this photograph?
What is one question that you have about this photograph?

This activity can be used for a number of purposes to improve students' critical thinking skills and inferential reading abilities. In the past, I have used this activity to enhance students' background knowledge of historical contexts for fiction, nonfiction, and poetry. For example, prior to reading an expository text on the work of Dorothea Lange, my sixth-grade students and I analyzed her famous photographs on the conditions for migrant worker families during the Great Depression. When teaching *The Diary of Anne Frank* and *The Book Thief*, I have used this lesson with (age appropriate) images from the Holocaust, including examples of Nazi propaganda that were used to persuade the citizens of Germany. Nancy has also used this lesson with her eighth-grade students, presenting photographs of Selma, Alabama, during the Civil Rights Movement in her thematic "Power of Words" unit. While this activity specifically mentions the use of photographs, I have also used paintings from the Harlem Renaissance as a way for students to anticipate the poetry of Langston Hughes. Not limited to reading comprehension, this activity can also be used to help spark students' imaginations at the start of creative writing unit. For example, students can rotate from photograph to photograph, gathering observations as inspiration to write a short story, or even incorporate vocabulary words from previous lessons to demonstrate a trifecta of proficiency in reading comprehension, writing, and vocabulary acquisition. In short, this lesson is versatile and lends itself to rich discussion and deep learning.

- Set up five stations with photographs at each interval. If using to establish historical context, a caption with each image may be helpful to help students understand what is happening in each photograph.
- Depending on your class, you can have students rotate at their own pace, or set a timer in order to keep them on task.
- Give each student a packet that contains five copies of **Reproducible 13D1: "Reading a Photograph."** Tell students that they are to look at each photograph closely and fill in each box with their observations on the people, places, things, and activities that appear in the photograph. They may use the guiding questions to help them develop their observations. This portion of the lesson may take two class periods.
- Once the students have recorded their observations, put them into groups for a "debriefing" session. Students should take turns sharing their notes, inferences, and questions.

- Regroup as a class and discuss students' responses to the photographs. It is interesting to see how students notice different aspects of the work.
- If time allows, project some of the photographs on the board and "annotate" the photographs, writing notes from the students' observations during the class debriefing.

Use **Reproducible 13D2: "Reading a Photograph" Exit Slip** to summarize the lesson.

Notes

1 Scriven & Paul, Summer 1987, p. 1.
2 Scriven & Paul, Summer 1987, p. 1.
3 Buckley, 2015.
4 Roth, 2010.
5 Gilbert, 2014.

Part VI

Achieving Teaching Goals
More Effectively

14

Help for Harried Teachers

"Being a community member is part of what it means to be authentic."[1] Seitel reinforces anthropologist Margaret Mead's famous view: "Never doubt that a small group of thoughtful, committed citizens can change the world; indeed it's the only thing that ever has."[2]

Most efforts to strengthen social and emotional skills in schools are designed to include all students, even though nearly 80% of the students do not have mental health problems. They also involve protective factors, such as "a positive and caring school climate, development of positive relationships between students and their teachers, and effective academic instructional planning."[3] The underlying idea here is one of synergy, where two interventions delivered simultaneously—in the home and in the school— have greater impact.

The focus of this chapter is to suggest actions that will connect you with:

- People in similar positions of authority—parents, caregivers, teachers, and administrators.
- Researchers and writers who regularly share current information in education.
- National organizations striving to advance children's education and social and emotional well-being.
- Publications and additional resources to further your own learning and share with others.
- Strategies to enhance students' social and emotional skills in general.

Psychologist Shefali Tsabary advises:

True giving, which is fundamentally different from giving because it fills an empty space in your life and is therefore a form of neediness, comes from awareness of inner abundance. There is no giving if the inner well is dry. Authentic giving originates from a well that overflows.[4]

ACTIVITY 14A Reflect, Read, and Research

John Dewey's popular quote, "We do not learn from experience . . . we learn from reflecting on experience," provides educators with the first step to organizing their efforts. Margaret Mead's maxim, "Without reflection, we go blindly on our way, creating more unintended consequences, and failing to achieve anything useful,"[5] further supports Dewey's words. To avoid becoming harried, an educator's first task is to make time for reflection.

Educators today often reflect publicly with online blogging, YouTube videos, TED Talks, and podcasts. The advantage is that you receive feedback, which spurs more reflection and subsequent action.

Multiple books guide educators about reflection. Organizations such as the Association for Supervision and Child Development (ASCD) and the National Council of Teachers of English (NCTE) provide step-by-step guides, rationale, and research related to reflection. Here are two other examples:

Teach100

Teach100 ranks and scores hundreds of education blogs. This is a great resource for educators to review in order to "hear" the voices of other educators as they reflect on their craft and share their experiences and research.

Bam Radio

Bam Radio is an online resource that aims to "amplify the voices of the education village." This resource provides educators with access to education podcasts, blog posts, and radio shows. Bam Radio also shares its reflections and research via its many platforms.

In addition to reflection, there are several internet resources that can assist you in lesson planning. Here are some of our favorite websites:

CommonLit.org

A free database of reading passages, guiding questions, and assessments organized by grade level, genre, and theme. This is a helpful resource if you are designing thematic units and are looking to assign selections across genres.

NewsELA.com

This website features nonfiction instructional content on current events that teachers can customize based on the reading levels of students in their classes. The site also has a collection specifically tailored to teach SEL competencies.

National Writing Project: www.nwp.org

An organization that promotes best practices in helping students develop 21st-century skills through written communication. They offer programs and a wealth of resources to help support teachers of writing.

ThisIBelieve.org

A tried and true-tested resource, ThisIBelieve.org offers students the opportunity to read, reflect, and formulate their own personal beliefs. This project has helped several of our students improve their self-awareness, social awareness, and responsible decision-making skills.

ACTIVITY 14B Establish a Professional Learning Network (PLN)

Thanks to the numerous social networking sites such as Facebook, Twitter, Voxer, and Instagram, many educator support groups exist solely online. Such groups provide forums for educators to come together around one or more common interests regardless of geographical location and offer rich opportunities for sharing ideas, advice, and resources.

Many websites feature discussion and/or messaging boards so that visitors to the site can discuss information, concerns, and opinions. These boards range from those that function like bulletin boards, where visitors post messages that others can see (one-way communication) to discussion forums that occur in *asynchronous* or *synchronous* fashion. An asynchronous discussion forum means that visitors can post comments or questions at any time, and someone can respond at another time. Synchronous discussion forums occur at specific times when participants can post and respond in the moment, often bringing people into contact from around the world.

One of the most obvious sources for support and validation for educators is other educators. A relationship with even one other teacher is all that it takes to reduce your own anxiety and elevate your craft. There are many opportunities to meet other teachers, including virtual and real time groups inside and outside the school community. The following sites are popular places for educators and others to explore, and most do not require any fees for the use of their platforms:

Facebook: www.facebook.com

Once you have established a free Facebook account, you can look to the "Groups" link on the left-hand menu. There are icons to "Create Group" and "Find New Groups," and you are able to adjust your privacy settings (e.g., who can see your personal information) by clicking on the icon that looks like a padlock with three little lines. The site is user-friendly, and there are also many online tips available outside of the Facebook site for those who have the time and inclination to explore the internet for Facebook-inspired ideas.

Pinterest: www.pinterest.com

This site functions like an interactive bulletin board, allowing users to "pin" websites to their own accounts. For example, suppose you search for "healthy snacks" and find a recipe for creative school snacks. To save this recipe, you may "pin" it to your "board." You are able to create your boards, almost like file folders, where your different pinned websites are available as snapshots for you to look at. You are also able to "follow" friends and others on Pinterest, and can therefore connect with others around specific interests or activities. There are numerous sites to explore related to teaching on Pinterest, featuring tips, humor, and forums for exchange.

Edmodo: www.edmodo.com

This site is specifically designed to bring teachers, families, and students together in the spirit of sharing. This site is particularly useful for professionals—teachers and administrators. Edmodo is a secure website that offers many opportunities for engagement. The detailed set of instructions walks users through the process of connecting with others on a specific topic or for continued professional development.

Twitter: https://twitter.com

Thousands of educators have Twitter accounts and regularly share information via Twitter chats and tweets. Popular Twitter chats can be found via www.iste.org/explore/articledetail?articleid=7

Educators generally post their picture, a link to their blog and/or website, and a short description of their professional work and personal interests. They share links to good ideas, blog posts, images, video, and other educational resources, ideas, and questions related to good teaching.

Discovery Education: www.discoveryeducation.com

This is a popular education site that has numerous teaching/learning resources and an online community of educators that eagerly share ideas.

Voxer: https://web.voxer.com/login

Many educators exchange ideas on this audial social media thread. Similar to Twitter and Facebook, Voxer provides educators with a place to share ideas. It's unique in that the ideas are shared via speaking rather than writing or sharing images. Many educators prefer this vehicle.

Google+: http://plus.google.com

Google+ is Google's social network. It is a network that is easily coordinated with the Google apps and accounts that you establish. Similar to Facebook and Twitter, Google+ consists of a stream of updates, conversations, and shared contact. You add your contacts to "circles," which provides a way to categorize and organize people. You may comment on people's share and also utilize the "Hangout" feature to video chat. There's a smartphone Google+ app as well.

ACTIVITY 14C Education Publications

Many organizations provide links to publications and resources that you may find useful and want to share with colleagues, relatives, and other learning community members:

The Inner Resilience Program: www.innerresilience-tidescenter.org/publications.html

Schools That Learn: http://schoolsthatlearn.com

Mindful Schools: www.mindfulschools.org

Edutopia: www.edutopia.org

MindShift said: ww2.kqed.org/mindshift/

Classroom Q&A With Larry Ferlazzo: http://blogs.edweek.org/teachers/
classroom_qa_with_larry_ferlazzo/

ACTIVITY 14D Get Involved in National and International Organizations

One of the quickest ways to get connected to others is by asking, "How can I get involved?" For example, the Bill and Melinda Gates Education Organization issued a request for proposals (RFP) for educators who wanted to host educator gatherings to Celebrate and Elevate Effective Teaching and Teachers in the United States. The events fostered collegiality, idea share, and support for educators. Education-related organizations and companies throughout the country support countless educator events that support teachers who want to get involved. Being able to help others very often results in helping oneself:

- Establish a network of responsible, reliable education supporters who are interested in working with teachers and schools.
- Form after-school clubs related to specific content areas.
- Connect adults in professional clubs, workshops, and courses to create and/or build teaching/learning efforts in that area.
- Inspire advocacy and activism for professional endeavor. Work with local governmental, community, and/or union groups.
- Write proposals for grants and to provide professional learning workshops and conference sessions related to the content areas you are most interested in.

For detailed tips and guidelines for starting your own local support group, see the Edmodo website (www.edmodo.com). The national organizations listed provide support and outreach in this area. Most of these national organizations have local affiliations in each state and outside of the United States as well.

Collaborative for Academic, Social, and Emotional Learning (CASEL): www.casel.org

Twitter: @caselorg

The leading organization in the United States for promoting SEL in preschool through high school, CASEL bases its advice entirely on evidence obtained in highly rigorous, widely respected research studies. The organization focuses its efforts and impact on research and policy.

ASCD: The Whole Child: www.ascd.org

Twitter: @ASCD

The Association for Supervision and Child Development is an international presence in curriculum development, designed to empower educators, promote leadership, and support success for individual and group learners.

National Center on Safe and Supportive Learning Environments (NCSSLE): http://safesupportivelearning.ed.gov

Twitter: @SSLearn

The NCSSLE addresses issues such as bullying, harassment, violence, and substance abuse in an effort to improve learning conditions for all students. Funded by the US Department of Education, this organization provides training to students, teachers, communities, families, and administrators at various levels.

Character Education Partnership: http://character.org

Twitter: @CharacterDotOrg

This nonprofit organization envisions young people everywhere as educated, inspired, ethical, engaged citizens. Offering training, a national conference, and evaluation tools, the organization strives to connect educators and others who seek to improve school conditions.

National Parent-Teacher Association: www.pta.org

Twitter: @NationalPTA

For over 100 years, National PTA has been recognized as the premier organization that connects stakeholders in children's educational experiences—families, students, teachers, administrators, and community members. The work of the National PTA and its partners is promoted through publications, conferences, and social media venues.

National Institute of Mental Health: www.nimh.nih.gov

Twitter: @NIMHgov

Dedicated to transforming the understanding and treatment of mental illnesses, this national organization supports and disseminates research on a variety of topics. Scientific perspectives and applications of numerous findings are presented in links to publications, blogs, and video clips.

National Education Association: www.nea.org

This is a national teachers' union that has countless links to online communities for teacher connection, learning, and opportunity.

National Council of Teachers of English (NCTE): www.ncte.org

This is the organization that supports teaching and learning in the area of English Language Arts.

Yale Center for Emotional Intelligence

A center that conducts research and offers teachers sample activities and lesson plans that support them in implementing SEL practices in their classroom.

International Society for Technology in Education (ISTE): www.iste.org

A global community of educators supporting the use of technology to teach and learn.

National Board of Professional Teaching Standards (NBPTS): www.nbpts.org

This national board works to strengthen the teaching profession and improve student learning by establishing high standards for teachers in American schools. Obtaining NBPTS certification promotes extensive educator reflection which leads to improved teaching, learning, and professional connections.

Center for Teaching Quality (CTQ): www.teachingquality.org

CTQ is a research-based, nonprofit advocacy organization that focuses primarily on the conditions of teaching with the vision of a high-quality public education system for all students, driven by the bold ideas and expert practices of teachers. Their mission is to connect, ready, and mobilize teacher/leaders to transform schools.

ACTIVITY 14E Take Advantage of Professional Learning Seminars and Conferences

There are countless professional learning seminars and conferences hosted by educational organizations, local school systems, universities, and other professional organizations. Most of these conferences and seminars can be discovered via your professional learning network (PLN), professional organizations, and school affiliations. Educators have the opportunity to attend and/or present at these organizations. To present, proposals are due about six months prior to the conference. Proposals are met with a selection process and applicants are notified if their proposal was accepted or not about one to three months prior to the conference.

ACTIVITY 14F Professional Grants

Professional organizations as well as local, state, and national professional and civic organizations offer grant funds to educators whose ideas meet the standards set by the organization. An internet search of local funding sources will result in multiple grant opportunities. Generally, grant applications are due about six months to one year prior to acceptance.

ACTIVITY 14G Building School Support

Developing trust, promoting a caring community that welcomes and respects differences, fostering cooperation and companionship, and otherwise creating a humane climate—these are all goals that most schools support. Furthermore, the majority of schools engage in ongoing self-evaluation to see how well the school is meeting these goals. These initial meetings provide opportunities for educators and school administrators to:

- Get to know each other.
- Explore shared interests and goals.
- Establish shared priorities for the school.
- Focus efforts on SEL.

Also, administrators work with teachers to integrate SEL principles and strategies. Setting high expectations for students, staff, and families is a means of expressing care. Many school districts throughout the world have articulated SEL as a priority in response to threats in their communities.[6] A recent publication of the International Academy of Education (IAE)—an organization that offers "timely syntheses of research-based evidence of international importance"—features the statement:

> Indeed, schools worldwide must give children intellectual and practical tools they can bring to their classrooms, families, and communities.

Social-emotional learning provides many of these tools. It is a way of teaching and organizing classrooms and schools that help children learn a set of skills needed to manage life tasks successfully, such as learning, forming relationships, communicating effectively, being sensitive to others' needs and getting along with others.[7]

As an engaged educator, your efforts may include bringing organizations such as the IAE to the attention of educational decision-makers and the general public in your community. Educated citizens' votes and actions can make a real difference in the lives of children.

Similarly, fostering service learning initiatives at your school will help students to foster SEL skills and knowledge by helping others in creative ways. Service learning empowers students to utilize academic skills to learn about situations of need and then to respond to those needs with collaborate efforts to serve others in the school, home, or community.

Lastly, one of the best ways to develop professionally is to read books specifically tailored to your educational interests, this book on SEL being one of them. Here is a comprehensive list of "greatest hits" that we ELA teachers have found helpful over the years:

Curriculum Design and Instruction

Falling in Love With Close Reading: Lessons for Analyzing Texts—and Life

Christopher Lehman and Kate Roberts

Comprehension and Collaboration

Stephanie Harvey and Harvey Daniels

Comprehension Going Forward

Ellin Oliver Keene & others

Content-Area Conversations

Douglas Fisher, Nancy Frey, and Carol Rothenberg

The Continuum of Literacy Learning

Gay Pinnell and Irene Fountas

Words, Words, Words

Janet Allen

Summarization in Any Subject

    Rick Wormeli

Classroom Instruction That Works

    Ceri Dean & others

Content Area Writing

    Harvey Daniels, Steven Zemelman, and Nancy Steinke

Teaching Reading in the Content Area

    Rachel Billmeyer and Mary Lee Barton

Words Their Way

    Francine Johnston & others

Notice and Note Signposts

    Kylene Beers

Notice and Note Nonfiction

    Kylene Beers

The Understanding by Design

    Grant Wiggins and Jay McTighe

So What Do They Really Know

    Cris Tovani

Writing Pathways

    Lucy Calkins

Building Academic Vocabulary

    Robert Marzano

Bringing Words to Life: Robust Vocabulary Instruction (First or Second Edition)

    Isabel L. Beck, Margaret G. McKeown, and Linda Kucan

Inside Words

    Janet Allen

Read, Write, Teach

Linda Rief

Work/Life Balance for Teachers

The Together Teacher

Maia Heyck-Merlin

Mindfulness

Mindfulness for Teachers

Tish Jennings

The Mindful Teacher

Dennis Shirely and Elizabeth MacDonald

Mindful Teaching and Teaching Mindfulness

Deborah Schoeberlein

Recommended Young Adult Books by SEL Type[8]

Self-Awareness

Like No Other, Una LaMarche

Neighboring teenagers are worlds apart in this modern-day romance. While recognizing their own changing perspectives, Jax and Devorah must navigate their feelings for each other. A refreshingly honest look at growing into your true self while honoring family expectations, questioning established belief systems, and battling cultural pressures.

The Beginning of Everything, Robyn Schneider

Who *are* you when you're not who you *were*? After a life-altering car accident, Ezra Faulkner must rediscover himself. Everyone knows him as the star tennis player with a popular girlfriend and a promising future. After the accident he has to figure out who to become when he can't be what everyone expects him to be.

A Monster Calls, Patrick Ness (*New York Times* bestseller and winner of the Carnegie Medal)

Conor's resistance to emotions impacts him both at home and in school. At home, Conor's mother is dying; at school, he is taunted by bullies. Each night, he finds himself haunted by a monster who takes the form of a giant yew tree. Is the monster real or a manifestation of his greatest fear?

Self-Management

The Thing About Jellyfish, Ali Benjamin (*New York Times* bestseller and 2015 National Book Award finalist)

Suzy struggles to deal with the death of her best friend in this heartbreakingly candid middle-grade novel. As she tries to make sense of a catastrophic loss, both the inviting world of fantasy and the safety of scientific facts offer Suzy ways to manage.

The War that Saved My Life, Kimberly Brubaker Bradley (2016 Newbery Honor book and winner of the 2016 Schneider Family Book Award)

Set in the tenements of war-torn London, Ada and her younger brother lead a claustrophobic existence under their abusive mother; yet, somehow, they know there is more. This story celebrates the power of motivation and love, proving we can overcome adversity and become our best self when we have a place to belong.

Twerp, Mark Goldblatt (Junior Library Guild Selection Bankstreet Best Book of the Year)

Meet Julian Twerski, a good kid who makes one horrible mistake. When Julian's English teacher asks him to keep a journal and reflect on his decisions, readers experience the consequences that result from poor impulse control, the pressures of adolescence, and the desperate desire to fit in.

Social Awareness

Mockingbird, Kathryn Erskine (National Book Award winner)

For students struggling to be patient and kind to peers on the autism spectrum, this book is a must-read. Caitlin, the main character, has Asperger's, and readers experience her frustration as she navigates a world of unfamiliar emotions and confusing "rules." Caitlin also lost her brother in a school shooting, providing teachers and parents with a relatively safe pathway to conversations about difficult topics.

Backlash, Sarah Darer Littman

A disturbing and raw look at how the lure of social media impacts our decision-making process. Lara and Bree are former best friends navigating the social pyramid of high school when the temptation to manipulate the other becomes too much. The internet is permanent; there are some things you can't take back, even if you hit delete. This book is both incredibly relatable and highly engaging.

Traffick, Ellen Hopkins

This verse novel tells the story of five teens victimized by sex trafficking. Gut-wrenching and poignant, the scenarios depicted are realistic without being graphic.

Lily and Dunkin, Donna Gephart (YALSA 2017 Best Fiction for Young Adults, YALSA 2017 Quick Picks for Reluctant Young Adult Readers, and ALA 2017 Rainbow Book List—GLBTQ Books)

Lily is a transgender girl and Dunkin is a boy coping with bipolar disorder. Together they navigate complex family dynamics, the bullies of middle school, and the challenges of life outside of "normal." Readers' hearts will ache for Lily and Dunkin, but rest assured that the tone is one of acceptance and hope.

The Hate U Give by Angie Thomas (William C. Morris Award winner, Printz Honor Book, Coretta Scott King Honor Book, #1 *New York Times* bestseller)

Starr Carter is 16 when she witnesses the shooting death of her childhood friend Khalil. Khalil is unarmed when shot and killed by a police officer at a traffic stop. The shooting becomes national news. Was Khalil a gangbanger thug or an innocent victim? The world wants to know what really happened, and Starr is the only one who knows. Can she find her voice?

Relationship Skills

The You I've Never Known, Ellen Hopkins

Ariel has lived alone with her dad for as long as she can remember. After 17 years of new homes, new schools, and new people, she is ready to settle down. Maya is a teenager who runs away from an abusive mother into the arms of an abusive older man. Ariel's and Maya's stories collide and raise questions about truth and the nature of love.

Letters to the Lost, Brigid Kemmerer

Juliet and Declan have an open and honest relationship. They tell each other their deepest thoughts and are vulnerable and honest in the letters they exchange. One little thing: their notes are anonymous; they don't really know the identity of the other person. Can we set aside judgments and preconceived notions and accept other people as they are? Bonus points to this novel for exploring perfectly imperfect family dynamics.

The Crossover, Kwame Alexander (2015 Newbery Medal winner and 2015 Coretta King Honor winner)

Josh and Jordan lead a pretty charmed life: they have great friends, relatively cool parents, and crazy-good basketball skills run in their blood. But sometimes bad things happen to good people. This book helps students understand that even the strongest among us need to ask for help. Readers will devour this verse novel in one sitting.

Decision-Making

The Perfect Score, Rob Buyea

The sixth graders in Mrs. Woods's class have enough to worry about, without state assessments looming over their heads. Told in multiple voices, this novel takes an honest look at what happens when positive intentions go awry. A wonderful story about ethical responsibility, showing students that even when we have a really good reason—even when our actions are justified—we still must consider every outcome of our decisions and face the consequences.

Notes From the Midnight Driver, Jordan Sonnenblick

Alex is your typical sarcastic, ungrateful teenager and, thanks to his parents' divorce, he's an angry one, too. After he crashes the family car, Alex is sentenced to community service at a local nursing home. This highly readable novel offers a realistic look at how young adults can redeem themselves after a stupid mistake and reminds us all that we are better than our worst day.

The Trouble in Me, Jack Gantos

When he meets his new neighbor, the desire to belong trumps Jack's ability to effectively analyze the consequences of his own decisions. How far will

Jack go? Not for the faint of heart, this autobiographical story lays it all on the table.

And finally, we'd like to add the following table.

SEL in the ELA Classroom: At a Glance

Here is a "Look for Tool," according to which the following strategies either incorporate the listed SEL competencies and/or help students develop them.[9]

Classroom Environment Activities

STRATEGY/ACTIVITY	Self-Awareness	Self-Management	Social Awareness	Building Relationships	Decision-Making
Student involvement in class norms	X	X	X	X	X
Acknowledge/reflect on feelings/mood at beginning of class	X				
Anonymous poll/ survey on opinions/ perspectives	X		X		X
Practice positive self-talk	X	X			
Establish a mistake-safe environment	X	X		X	
Promote growth mindset concepts/skills	X	X			X
Peer tutoring	X	X		X	
Practice active listening	X	X	X	X	X
Use accountable talk	X	X	X	X	X
Identify common values	X		X		X
Establish respect for varying perspectives/ cultures	X	X	X	X	
Problem-solving strategies	X	X			X
Mindfulness strategies	X	X	X	X	X

Group work activities

STRATEGY/ACTIVITY	Self-Awareness	Self-Management	Social Awareness	Building Relationships	Decision-Making
Cooperative learning (structured)	X	X	X	X	X
Turn and talk	X	X	X	X	
Think-pair-share	X	X	X	X	
Group project (includes individual accountability)	X	X	X	X	X
Socratic seminar	X	X	X	X	X
Provide exemplars to ensure student understanding of major assignments	X	X			X
Think aloud	X	X	X		
Peer editing	X	X	X	X	X
Reading buddies	X	X	X	X	X
Jigsaw	X	X	X	X	X

SEL and Assignments

Reflect on prior knowledge before activity	X				
Compare/contrast feelings and experiences with those of character or historical figure	X		X		
Autobiography/journal writing	X		X		
Goal setting for projects, grades, etc.	X	X			X
Keep prediction chart during reading assignment	X		X		X
Venn diagrams	X		X		X
Read texts/articles with opposing views	X	X	X	X	X
Debates	X	X	X	X	X
Discuss current events	X		X		
Stories from different cultural viewpoints	X		X		
Role play/skits	X	X	X	X	X
Exit tickets	X	X	X		
Writing conferences	X	X	X	X	X

Notes

1 Seitel, 2009.
2 Mead, cited in Seitel, 2009.
3 Merrell & Gueldner, 2010, pp. 104–105.
4 Tsabary, 2010, p. 181.
5 Mead, cited in Seitel, 2009.
6 CASEL, 2014.
7 Elias, 2003.
8 Special thanks to Franklin, Massachusetts, reading specialists Mary Cotillo and Erin O'Leary.
9 A special thank you to Dr. Victoria Ekk, curriculum coordinator for the North Attleborough Public Schools, Massachusetts, for creating and sharing this resource with the authors of this book.

15

Multiple Means of Measuring Your Students' SEL[1]

For the immediate future, the evaluation of social/emotion instruction is going to be based on a combination of measures. The most prominent index will be an increase in academic learning (AL), as presented and scored by computers. This is because AL is still the preeminent goal of most schools, universally. That is changing, however.[2]

The following table presents strategies that already exist. It is likely that in the near future, electronic devices for both teaching and testing SEL will be available to all students, regardless of the economic state of the school system. This will further enhance SEL in the schools. Let us examine this list in terms of its established characteristics, as well as the authors' endorsement (or lack of it) as to the acceptable utility of each type.

Types of In-School SEL Measurement

As to oft-criticized self-report surveys, we quote measurement experts: The argument for them rests upon at least three pillars:

1. As researchers Angela Duckworth and David Yeager have written, "self-report questionnaires are arguably better suited than any other measure for assessing internal psychological states, like feelings

Type of Measurement	Instrument name	URL	Age range	Computer Scoring
1 Direct observation of student behaviors		http://hepg.org/her-home/issues/harvard-educational-review-volume-74-issue-3	3–18	Not endorsed
2 Behavior rating scales	DESSA SEARS Devereux Early Childhood Assessment for Preschoolers	http://kaplanco.com or http://studentstrengths.org http://strongkids.oregon.edu/ http://SEARS.htm http://centerforresilientchildren.org/home/dcrc-resources/	6–15 3–18 3–5	Machine scorable Endorse Do not endorse Do not endorse
3 Self-report instruments*	BERS DAP EQI-YV SEI-YV Youth Emotional Intelligence SEI Brain Profiles SEARCH Survey	http://proedinc.com http://search-institute.org http://mhs.com http://6seconds.org/tools/sei/ http://6seconds.org/tools/sei/ http://search-institute.org/surveys/REACH?gclid=CMyJ9pPx-NACFcKPswodIcYLlg	3–18 6–18 5–13 7–18 7–18 13–18	Machine scorable, endorsed Machine scorable, endorsed Machine scorable, endorsed Machine scorable, Endorsed Machine scorable, Endorsed Do not endorse
4 Correct answer techniques	Remote Associates test, A and B.	Seymour Mednick; http://remote-associates-test.com/	A = 6–13, B = 14–18	Machine scorable, endorsed
5 Projective/expressive techniques	Draw-a-family, ink blot	http://creativecounseling101.com/kinetic-family-drawing-test-art-therapy.html http://theinkblot.com/	3–18 3–18	Do not endorse Do not endorse
6 Interview techniques	Ask students probing questions at their knowledge of SEL		3–18	Do not endorse

Measure	Notes/examples	Reference/URL	Age	Scoring/endorsement
7 Open-answer technique or essay evaluation	1. "Two-string test" 2. Fill in Xs	http://books.google.com/books?id=cpc7CJH1-s8C&pg=PA762&lpg=PA762&dq=Two-string+test+of+creativity&source A. Maslow http://markrunco.com	6–18 3–18	Machine scorable, endorsed Machine scorable, endorsed
8 Fluency of examples, e.g., # of instances of self-control	Describe times when student has employed SEL		3–18	Example count
9 Instances of criminal behavior, e.g., weapons found			3–18	Count # in summary report, with severity rating
10 Antisocial behavior counts, e.g., verbal fights	Or brandishing a weapon on school property			School reports by classroom
11 Analyses of drawings: counting and pattern recognition	See Haney, Russell, and Bebell (Fall 2004)		3–18	Machine matching to templates; endorse
12 School attendance records by classroom				Tallies of change in daily school attendance, after-school clubs and sports participation, pep rallies, etc.
13 Teacher behavior	Responsive practices: modeling, scaffolding, facilitating, and coaching	http://measuringsel.casel.org/observational-data-inspire-sel-practice/	3–18	Classroom observers (retired educators, trained high schoolers)
14 Shadow benefits	See Belfield and others (2015)	Columbia's Center for Benefit-Cost Studies	3–18	Reduction in societal costs directly resulting from SEL
15 School satisfaction survey		http://education.stateuniversity.com/pages/2392/School-Climate.html		School, classroom specific
16 Qualitative formative assessment		www.edutopia.org/blog/building-sel-skills-formative-assessment-robert-marzano	3–18	Not endorsed at this time
17 Academic Learning (AL) objective scores[3]	E.g., Great Teachers and Leaders	http://gtlcenter.org/technical-assistance/professional-learning-modules/scoring-student-learning-objectives	6–18	Endorse

* Please see our quotation about self-report measures, below.

of belonging." A large body of research has shown that those psychological states can powerfully influence important educational outcomes such as grades, high school graduation rates, and college enrollment rates.

2. Self-report surveys are efficient and cost-effective when compared to other ways of measuring SEL.

3. Youth voice and perspective matter. Youth self-report surveys are an important tool for capturing and understanding young people's lived experiences from their own perspectives.

That said, self-report SEL measures have several limitations. Researchers must address these in the design of survey instruments, and practitioners should be aware of them when using data from those instruments. One of the most important of those limitations is "reference bias," or the fact that people often judge themselves and the world based upon their own experiences and understanding. As a result, responses can be highly subjective, making it difficult to interpret the data when comparing across participants. For example, what one student considers working hard, another might consider doing the bare minimum.

In surveys we design, we use several approaches to minimize or mitigate reference bias. For example, we conduct cognitive interviews (or survey "Think Alouds") with youth who are similar to those we seek to include in the study. In these interviews, young people help us understand how young people may differ in their interpretation of a survey item. We then use this information to refine the survey. In addition, we rarely ask youth to compare themselves to others.[4]

One of these measurement methods in the preceding table is of particular interest: the open-answer technique (#7 in the table) and in particular, the "two-string" test (#7.1 in the table).[5] This approach meets the criteria of allowing open-ended typed answers to be identified as correct or incorrect. Here is how that happens, using the "two-string" test of creative problem solving as an exemplar.

ACTIVITY 15A Open-Ended Typed Answers to Creativity Test

Materials Needed: A wide empty room or space; two medium-weight strings; length of each equals 1 foot shorter than the distance from floor to ceiling (12 feet high at most). The two strings are attached firmly to the ceiling, 14 feet apart. The simple goal is to tie the two strings together. As you can

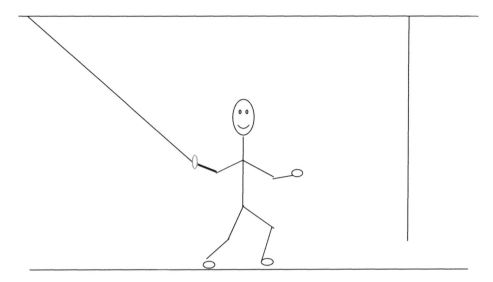

Figure 15.1

see in Figure 15.1, even the tallest person, holding one string, can only move about 8 feet toward the other string, and thus cannot reach it. As a possible aid: a mousetrap.

Start by attaching the two strings to the ceiling of a room, as in Figure 15.1. With a 10-foot ceiling, each string would be 9 feet long. They are 14 feet apart.

Tell the students: Your goal is simply to tie the two strings together. One item is available for your use in finding the solution—a mousetrap. Standing between the two strings, you should try to figure out how to tie them together, with or without the mousetrap. No matter how tall you are, you will not be able to reach the two strings, even if you try using the mousetrap to extend your reach. Do you think you can do it? The solution appears at the bottom of this page.[6]

Many people are unable to reach this solution because they do not imagine mousetraps being used for something other than for catching mice. Here's an example of what we mean: a graduate student in psychology studied the problem and said, "I've got it! The answer is the mousetrap. You catch a bunch of mice until you get one that isn't seriously hurt. You make a pet of it, then train it to be a 'trapeze' mouse. It will jump up on one of the strings and pump back and forth until it is able to swing it over to you while you are holding the other string!" This is a good example of *functional fixity*: this student believed that a mousetrap's only function is to capture mice. His solution could conceivably work, but it is much more complicated than simply using the trap as a weight.

Most significantly, in over 3,000 ADministrations of the two-string test,[7] every right answer contained the word "swing," and none of the wrong answers did. In a solvable social or emotional test (has a right answer), any word which is always found in that right answer could be computer scored. This is true whether that word is seemingly relevant to the answer or not. As long as a computer model is able to pick out the important terms, it can classify high SEL answers, and distinguish them from those that are low in this capacity.

For example, suppose you wanted to reliably discriminate between student athletes who have learned social and emotional skills well, and those who have not. You might want to know this information in order to recognize which coaches are doing a good job of promoting SEL. If you could find a word or phrase that almost always appears in answers you consider correct, and almost never in wrong answers, that word or phrase would do an acceptable job of differentiating between the two.

In fact, you wouldn't even need to make a judgment of the students' answers. You might ask the regular teachers of a group of athletes to rank them on SEL. Then, if those who ranked high regularly use particular terms in each of their answers, and those ranked low don't, you have a set of questions that can be computer scored. Get enough of such questions and you have a valid instrument.

As you can see in this chapter, SEL evaluation has come a long way in recent years. Now if we can only get education's leaders to recognize the value of SEL itself.

Notes

1 Adapted from submission by Dacey to: *Harvard Educational Review, J. Neuro-education*
2 We dare to hope this book will contribute to that change!
3 Best method so long as AL predominates in the schools
4 Pekel, Roehlkepartain, & Syvertsen, April 11, 2018.
5 Krueger, 2016.
6 The mouse trap must be used to solve the problem. Attach it to one of the strings, then *swing* it away from you. Go grasp the other string, and when the first string swings back to you, catch it. The two strings may be tied together easily.
7 Dacey & Conklin, 2013.

16

The Future of SEL

So, the future of SEL. How can this book's authors foretell the future of this complex discipline? As you will see, most of the predictions offered in this chapter are based on new, research-based facts.[1] The rest result from educated hopefulness on our part. What is clear is that the beginnings of a tidal wave of support for SEL can be discerned in scholarly journals, professional blogs, newspaper articles, on the agenda of parent-teacher organizations, and in conversations along the sidelines at school sports events.[2] But for the present, there are some serious impediments, too.

For instance, in *5 Charts That Explain the Future of Education*,[3] Adam Shirley offers this one (Figure 16.1).

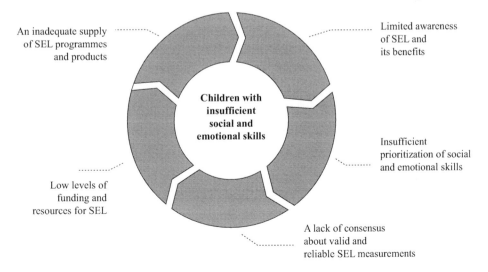

Figure 16.1

Of course, Shirley is talking about SEL as independent of AL. SEL *blended* with AL will soon be seen as much more important because:

- SEL will be recognized as more responsible for success in life than AL.
- When students experience a deficit in SEL, whether due to lack of opportunity to learn or because of psychopathology, they will inevitably suffer a deficit in AL. Educational leaders will insist on a more reasonable balance between the two.
- Most teachers know that they became professional educators more because they care about SEL than because they care about AL. Increasingly, they will begin to act on their distaste for "teaching to the test" and drilling children on facts.
- The majority of parents will come to understand that scores on the SAT tests correlate only with socioeconomic level. Such scores have little relation either to success in college or success in life.
- As a result, college admissions officers will de-emphasize quantitative measures such as SATs and school grades, and will find ways to assess potential students' social and emotional skills, which do predict superior performance in college and in life.
- The power of SEL will be supported not only from the standpoint of psychology, sociology, and educational theory, but also from physical data: benefits to the human hormonal and central nervous systems, as evidenced by blood cell analysis and functional magnetic resonance imaging (fMRI), i.e., neuro-science. Research on the workings of the amygdala in the brain will be especially prominent.
- The analysis and improvement of school social climate have become popular topics for study. The atmosphere in classrooms will continue to receive attention, which will in turn benefit SEL.
- The continued growth of family and school alliances will foster the success of SEL.
- SEL will find its way into college classrooms, especially those in the helping professions such as psychology and sociology, as well as in STEAM-related courses.
- It will also begin to move into the curricula of graduate programs, most especially psychotherapy, medicine, business, and education.[4]

Facilitation of SEL Goals

- Because, understandably, "if it's not tested, it's not taught," teacher assessment will devote a much more significant role to the evaluation and educator's ability to foster SEL (see previous chapter).
- The measurement of SEL will be based on a combination of tests presented and scored by humans and by computers. This will happen because in the foreseeable future, computers will continue to outperform humans in speed and memory, but humans will continue to outperform computers in pattern recognition, such as grasping handwriting and turning it into data. Groups of scholars are working on this aspect right now.[5]

Breathing to Tranquility

In a Spanish Harlem second grade class, I watched a session of "breathing buddies," part of the daily routine. One by one, each child took a small stuffed animal from a cubby, found a place to sit down, and put the animal on his or her belly. Then the children watched the animals go up on an in-breath, counting 1-2-3-4-5, and down on their out-breath, to the same count. This exercise, the teacher said, leaves them calm and focused for the rest of the day. This state is hard to imagine, given the tumultuous home lives the teacher ascribed to most of the second graders in his class.[6]

Return of the Arts

STEM (science, technology, engineering, and mathematics) is currently seen in many school systems as a unified subject matter area. In the future it will be known more broadly as "STEAM," with the A standing for the arts, such as drawing, art history, music, dance, and drama. The inclusion of arts in the STEM acronym is in recognition of the value of creativity. There will be teachers who specialize in the arts, and they will emphasize the role of SEL. In addition, the effect of studying the arts on other STEM subjects will become apparent. For example, those who do well in geometry will find they are better at painting, and vice versa.

Online SEL

Electronic devices of all kinds will become as ubiquitous as the blackboards and chalk of yesteryear. These devices will make possible the cultivation of SEL through such technologies as video clips, online idea boards, computers that read body language and facial expressions, and electronic simulations. Innovative strategies may include new virtual experience video games such as *The Sims* (seen as a female game) for boys, friendship movies such as *Hunger Games*, and religion-specific programs such as OWL[7] (*Our Whole Lives*, for teaching non-sectarian sexuality values). Most likely the major concern will be the repercussions of too much use of electronics: "ECAT: everyone connected, all the time."[8]

Non-classroom Settings for SEL

Much imaginative instruction will begin to take place outside of classrooms but within schools. For example, after-school, weekend, and summertime programs will be held on school property.[9] Some of this education will occur in schoolyard settings, such as Project Adventure's ropes courses, creativity projects, moral judgment exercises, socio-drama, and socially inspirational programs. Another innovation will be awards for actions that demonstrate social and emotional excellence. Students will be instructed that when they see extraordinarily humane behavior, they should report it to school authorities, who will reward it.

Non-school Settings for SEL

Some SEL will take place in settings other than school properties altogether. For example, infant assessments for social and emotional abilities will take place in clinics, so that young children who suffer deficits can receive remedial care. Formal mediation of actual student-student and teacher-student disputes may be held in a mediator's offices.

More Caring Citizens

As we have noted elsewhere in this book, there is evidence of a decline in the average person's caring for his fellow citizens. In particular, we have seen a worldwide waning of student interest in civic responsibility.[10] As the numbers of human beings have burgeoned, especially in the biggest of our cities, our caring for each other has dropped, perhaps as a defense mechanism.

It is tremendously important that this be rectified. We believe this will be one of the top priorities of future SEL. As Daniel Goleman puts it, "Recent studies suggest that the mammalian brain circuitry for caring, on which empathic concern depends, can be strengthened with the right training and that this, in fact, makes children kinder and more generous to others."[11]

Realism

> Now [in technology] we have low cost, small size and more bandwidth. But most importantly we have social systems. Like Facebook. And that's why VR [virtual reality], AR [augmented reality] and mixed reality will not only stay, but will change everything.
>
> —Robert Scoble

In Chapter 2 of this book, we explored the concept of authenticity. This trait will also characterize new aspects of SEL, especially of the digital variety. As Dr. Goleman puts it, teachers should "put their learners in the driving seat and then build decision points in a learning experience based on relevant situations and choices with the same instant feedback as you would receive in a game."[12] The current term for this is "gamification." One crucial attribute of most video games is increased user retention: just ask an 11-year-old about his favorite game, then be prepared to listen for a while! "When users remember the learned material, apply it to their real lives, and come back to learn more, you know your [gamification] project has been successful."[13]

Many games now rely on the newest electronic teachers: augmented and virtual reality. The difference between the two lies mainly in the gear. In the case of AR, the learner has an enhanced view of the material, making it more authentic. An example would be 3-D movies such as *Hugo* and *Avatar*. Both films would be excellent as SEL curricula, by the way. However, that user does not control what happens on his screen.

The most stunning aspect of the future of SEL will probably be virtual reality:

> But listen—a movie that gives one sight and sound. Suppose now I add taste, smell, even touch—is your interest taken by the story? Suppose I make it so that you are in the story, you speak to the shadows,

and the shadows reply, and instead of being on a screen, the story is all about you, and you are in it.

—Stanley Weinbaum, *Pygmalion's Spectacles*, 1935 (!)

Technologists are still working on smell and taste, but Weinbaum's "magic spectacles" eerily foreshadow the current prominence for 360-degree games, videos, and virtual worlds.[14] Google *Expeditions* is a fine exemplar. This app allows teachers and students to take "immersive virtual journeys," such as traveling to historical landmarks, diving underwater with sharks, and visiting outer space. It requires only a cell phone and a $9 cardboard viewer! Google plans to train teachers to use VR to enhance literacy (see edu.google.com/expeditions/#about). Fields outside of education are using VR to train professionals. For example, doctors are able to use VR to practice operations, and experience what it is like to live with a mental illness such as schizophrenia.

The Ultimate Innovation: Computer to Brain and Vice Versa

Everything about our world is going to change. And this means deep cultural change. The kind of change we saw in the 1960's when the electric guitar brought us rock'n'roll, when the pill brought us the sexual revolution, and when the space race brought us to the Moon and gave us the internet.

—Anders Emil Møller

This next quote may *seem* fanciful, but we will not be surprised to see it happen:

This week,[15] we got our first look at Neuralink, a new company cofounded by [Elon] Musk with a goal of building computers into our brains by way of "neural lace," a very early stage technology that lays on your brain and bridges it to a computer. It's the next step beyond even that blending of the digital and physical worlds, as human and machine become one.

Assuming the science works—and lots of smart people believe that it will—this is the logical endpoint of the road that smartphones started us on. If smartphones gave us access to information and augmented reality puts that information in front of us when we need it, then putting neural lace in our brains just closes the gap. Musk has said this is because the rise of artificial intelligence—which underpins a lot of the other technologies, including voice assistants and virtual reality—means humans will have to augment themselves just to keep up with the machines.

If you're curious about this idea, futurist Ray Kurzweil is the leading voice on the topic.[16]

More Research

There is one more area that we think will benefit SEL greatly: government and privately funded research. As we have pointed out in numerous places in this book, there is growing consensus among instructional leaders, activist parents and indeed the general public. The whole world needs to do a better job of fostering SEL, and that will mean carefully controlled experiments and evaluations. Throughout the 20th and so far in the 21st centuries, huge amounts of money have been spent on how to promote academic learning. Although SEL has suffered from an almost complete dearth of such support, we feel confident that this is about to change.

In summary, "Teaching SEL will become equally important [as AL], as our social media gradually changes too, further breaking down the barriers of location and communication."[17] We are seeing examples in the work of, for example, the excellent 6Seconds[18] program. This change is real, and that is why we believe AL embedded with SEL is, universally, the future of education. We hope our book will assist you in making this revolution take place.

Notes

1 Dusenbury & Weissberg, April 2017.
2 CASEL, 2016; Weissberg, 2016; Zakrzewski, 2015, p. 1.
3 Shirley, 2016, p. 1.
4 Goleman, 2016.
5 E.g., Lake, in press.
6 N. Bryan, personal communication.
7 UUA, 2018.
8 Kurzweil, 2012, p. 21.
9 Dacey, 1980.
10 Talloires, 2017.
11 Goleman, 2016, p. 593.
12 Coppens, 2016, p. 1.

13 Hughes, 2016, p. 1.
14 Weinbaum, 1935.
15 Weinberger, April 2, 2017.
16 Kurzweil, 2006 and 2012.
17 Lawrie, 2017, p. 1.
18 6Seconds.org, 2017.

Bibliography

AACAP. (2011). *Annual report*. Retrieved from aacap.org/App_Themes/AACAP/docs/about_us/annual_report/AACAP_2011_Annual_Report.pdf

American Meditation Society. (2018). *What is meditation?* americanmeditationsociety.org

ASCD. (2018). *Pathways to equity*. Retrieved from ascd.org/publications/educational-leadership/apr18/vol75/num07/Giving-Students-the-Right-Kind-of-Writing-Practice.aspx

Astin, J., & Shapiro, D. (2001). Measuring the psychological construct of control: Applications to transpersonal psychology. *International Journal of Stress Management*.

Baird, I. (2014). *A mindful cure to bullying*. Retrieved from www.huffingtonpost.com/izzy-baird/bullying_b_5591930.html

Bandura, A. (1994). Self-efficacy. In V. S. Ramachaudran (Ed.), *Encyclopedia of human behavior* (Vol. 4, pp. 71–81). New York, NY: Academic Press. (Reprinted in H. Friedman [Ed.], *Encyclopedia of mental health*. San Diego, CA: Academic Press, 1998).

Belfield, C., & others. (2015). *The economic value of social and emotional learning*. New York: Center for Benefit-Cost Studies in Education, Teachers College, Columbia University.

Bergland, C. (2016). *10 ways mindfulness and meditation promote well-being*. Retrieved from psychologytoday.com/blog/the-athletes-way/201504/10-ways-mindfulness-and-meditation-promote-well-being

Bethell, C.D., Newacheck, P., Hawes, E., & Halfon, N. (2014). Adverse childhood experiences: Assessing the impact on health and school engagement and the mitigating role of resilience. *Health Affairs*. December 2014, *33*(12), 2106–2115, doi:10.1377/hlthaff.2014.0914

Bloom, D. (2016). Instead of detention, these students get meditation. *CNN* (Cable News Network). Retrieved 16 April 2018 from http://cnn.com

Brooks, D. (2006, April 20). *Virtues and victims*. New York, NY: The NY Times.

Buckley, J., & others (2015). Defining and teaching evaluative thinking. *American Journal of Evaluation*, *36*(3), 375–388.

CASEL. (2016). *SEL research*. Retrieved from casel.org/research/#Field

CASEL. (2017, p. 1). *SEL research*. Retrieved from casel.org/research/#FieldGo to the store Select all Cressey, & others.

Center for Collaborative Education. (2017). *Beyond standardized tests: A new vision for assessing student learning and school quality*. Retrieved from http://cce.org/files/MCIEA-White-Paper_Beyond-Standardized-Tests.pdf

Clarebout, G., & others. (2010). The relations between self-regulation and the embedding of support in learning environments. *Educational Technology Research and Development*, *58*(5), 573–587.

Cohen, J. (Ed). (2001). *Caring classrooms, intelligent schools: The social emotional educa-tion of young children*. New York: Teachers College Press.

Coleman, J. (1969). *The adolescent society*. Glencoe, IL: Free Press.

Coppens, A. (2016). *What are the most effective uses of gamification in learning?* Retrieved from elearningindustry.com/free-ebooks/gamification-reshapes-learning

Cressey, J., Bettencourt, J., Donahue-Keegan, D., Villegas-Reimers, E., & Wong, C. (2017). *Social-emotional learning in teacher education: A needs assessment survey of teacher educators*. Boston, MA: Massachusetts Consortium for Social-Emotional Learning in Teacher Education.

Dacey, J. (1975a). Moral education. In J. Travers (Ed.), *The new children*. Hartford, CN: Greylock.

Dacey, J. (1975b, December). The camp school idea. *Learning*.

Dacey, J. (1976). *New ways to learn*. Hartford, CN: Greylock.

Dacey, J. (Ed.) (1980). *Where the world is: Teaching basic skills outdoors*. Santa Monica, CA: Goodyear.

Dacey, J. (1982). *Adult development*. Glenview, IL: Scott, Foresman.

Dacey, J. (1986). *Adolescents today* (3rd ed.). Glenview, IL: Scott, Foresman.

Dacey, J. (1989a). *Fundamentals of creative thinking*. Lexington, MA: D. C. Heath/Lexington Books.

Dacey, J. (1989b). Peak periods of creative growth across the life span. *Journal of Creative Behavior, 23*(4), 224–247.

Dacey, J. (1989c). Discriminating characteristics of the families of highly creative adolescents. *Journal of Creative Behavior, 23*(4), 263–271.

Dacey, J. History of creativity. In *Encyclopedia of creativity* (3 Vols., 2nd ed.). San Francisco, CA: Academic Press.

Dacey, J. (In process with E. Bracher). *The freshman 15: 15 social and emotional assets for college success*.

Dacey, J. (In process). *Funnier than dirty*.

Dacey, J. (In process). Why don't you just relax?.

Dacey, J., & Conklin, W. (2013). *Creativity and the standards*. Huntington Beach, CA: TCM/Shell.

Dacey, J., & Fiore, L. (2000). *Your anxious child*. San Francisco, CA: Jossey-Bass/Wiley.

Dacey, J., & Fiore, L. (2006). *The safe child handbook: How to protect your family and cope with anxiety in a threat-filled world*. New York, NY: Wiley.

Dacey, J., & Lennon, K. (1998). *Understanding creativity: The interplay of biological, psychological and social factors*. San Francisco, CA: Jossey-Bass/Wiley.

Dacey, J., & Packer, A. (1992). *The nurturing parent*. New York, NY: Simon & Schuster.

Dacey, J. & Ripple, R. (1969). Relationships of some adolescent characteristics and verbal creativity. *Psychology in the Schools, 6*(3): 321–324.

Dacey, J., & Weygint, L. (2002). *The joyful family*. San Francisco, CA: Conari.

Dacey, J., Amara, D., & Seavey, G. (1993, Winter). Reducing dropout rate in inner city middle school children through instruction in self-control. *Research on Middle Level Education, 202*, 91–103.

Dacey, J., Criscitiello, G., & Devlin, M. (2017). *Integrating SEL into your curriculum: Activities and reproducibles for academic success, grades 3–5*. New York, NY: Routledge.

Dacey, J., deSalvatore, L., & Robinson, J. (1997). The results of teaching middle school students two relaxation techniques as part of a conflict prevention program. *Research on Middle Level Education, 20*(2), 91–102.

Dacey, J., Fiore, L., & Brion-Meisels, S. (2016, May). *Your child's social and emotional well-being*. Chichester, UK: Houghton-Mifflin/Wiley.

Dacey, J., Kenny, M., & Margolis, D. (2008). *Adolescent development* (3rd ed.). New York, NY: Cengage Learning.

Dacey, J., Mack, M., & Fiore, L. (2016, May). *Your anxious child* (2nd ed.). Chichester, UK: Wiley.

Dacey, J., Neves, L., & Tripp, N. (2018). *Integrating SEL into your curriculum: Activities and reproducibles for academic success, grades 6–8*. New York, NY: Routledge.

Dacey, J., Travers, J., & Fiore, L (2009). *Human development across the lifespan* (7th ed.). New York, NY and Boston, MA: McGraw-Hill.

Das, K. (2013). *The quantum guide to life: How the laws of physics explain our lives from laziness to love*. New York, NY: Skyhorse.

Datta, N. (2016). *Positive thinking: How to foster in your child*. Retrieved from aboutkidshealth.ca/En/HealthAZ/FamilyandPeerRelations/life-skills/Pages/Positive-thinking-How-to-foster-iin-your-child.aspx

de Bruin, A. B., Thiede, K. W., & Camp, G. (2001). Generating keywords improves metacomprehension and self-regulation in elementary and middle school children. *Journal of Experimental Child Psychology, 109*(3), 294–310.

Dilipkumar, D. (2017). *Generative adversarial image refinement for handwriting recognition*. Student dissertation. Retrieved from ml.cmu.edu/research/dap-papers/F17/dap-dilipkumar-deepak.pd

Doll, J. (2017). *How to combat your anxiety, one step at a time*. Retrieved from nytimes.com/2017/12/21/smarter-living/how-to-combat-your-anxiety-one-step-at-a-time.html

Donahue-Keegan, D. (2017, June 5). *Conference: Boston & beyond, PEAR*.

Dredge. (2018). *About*. Retrieved from dredgecam.com/home

Dusenbury, L., & Weissberg, R. (April 2017). *Social emotional learning in elementary school: Preparation for success*. University Park, PA: Robert Wood Johnson Foundation/Penn State.

Dusenbury, L., & others. (2015). The case for preschool through high school state learning standards for SEL. In J. A. Durlak & others (Eds.), *Handbook of social and emotional learning*. New York, NY: Guilford Press.

Dweck, C. (2006). Mindset: What does this mean for me. In C. Dweck (Ed.), *MindSet: A book written by Carol. Teaching a growth mindset creates motivation and productivity in the worlds of business, education, and sports*. Retrieved from mindsetonline.com/whatisit/whatdoesthismeanforme/index.html

Editor-in-chief. (2018, May 16). Opinion. *Boston Globe*.

EEOC. (2018). *Sexual harassment*. Retrieved from eeoc.gov/laws/types/sexual_harassment.cfm

Elias, M. J. (2003). *Academic and social-emotional learning*. Brussels, Belgium: International Academy of Education.

Elstad, E., & Turmo, A. (2010). Students' self-regulation and teacher's influence in science: Interplay between ethnicity and gender. *Research in Science & Technological Education, 28*(3), 249–260.

English, B. (2014, July 29). Workplace bullies. *The Boston Globe*, p. 12G.

Fiore, L., & Dacey, J. (2011). *Lifesmart*. New York, NY and Boston, MA: McGraw-Hill.

Flannick, J., et al. (2014). Loss-of-function mutations in SLC30A8 protect against type 2 diabetes. *Nature Genetics, 46*(4): 357–363.

Galinsky, E. (2010). *Mind in the making: The seven essential life skills every child needs*. NAEYC (special ed.). New York: HarperCollins.

Gallagher, P., & Kittle, K. (2018). Giving students the right kind of writing practice. *Educational Leadership, 75*(7), 14–20.

Gilbert, I. (2014). *Independent thinking*. Carmarthen, UK: Independent Thinking Press.

Goleman, D. (2016). *A force for good: The Dalai Lama's vision for our world*. New York, NY: Bantam Books.

Goleman, D., Boyatzis, R., & McKee. A. (2013). *Primal leadership: unleashing the power of emotional intelligence*. Cambridge, MA: Harvard Press.

Goodwin, B., & Hein, H. (2016). The X-factor in college success. *Educational Leadership, 73*(6), 77–78.

Goodwin, B., & Hein, H. (2018). Research Says/The X Factor in College Success. *Educational Leadership*. v73 n6 p77–78 Mar 2016.

Grimm, J., & Grimm, W. (1815). *Der Fuchs und das Pferd, kinder und hausmärchen*, vol. 2 (c), no. 46. (In later editions this tale is number 132.)

Haney, W., Russell, M., & Bebell, D. (2004, September). Drawing on education: Using drawings to document schooling and support change. *Harvard Educational Review, 74*(3), 241–272.

Henning , B., & others. (2015). The cortisol response to exercise in young adults. *Frontiers in Behavioral Neuroscience, 9*, 13.

Henry, O. (1909). The last leaf. *New York Sunday World Magazine*.

Huang, F. L., & Cornell, D. G. (2015). The impact of definition and question order on the prevalence of bullying victimization using student self-reports. *Psychological Assessment, 27*(4), 1484–1493.

Hughes. (2016). *What are the most effective uses of gamification in learning?* Retrieved from elearningindustry.com/how-gamification-reshapes-learning#andrew-hughes

Jagers, R. (2018). *Webinar: Equity and SEL: What educators need to know and do*. Retrieved from nys21cclc.org/event/webinar-equity-and-sel-what-educators-need-to-know-and-do/

Johnson, D., Johnson, R., & Stamme, B. (2000). *Cooperative learning methods: A meta-analysis*. Minneapolis, MN: University of Minnesota Press.

Jung, L. (2018). *From goals to growth*. Retrieved from ascd.org/publications/books/118032/chapters/Redefining-Student-Support.aspx

Kaufman, S. (2013). *Openness to experience is absolutely essential to creativity*. Retrieved from blogs.scientificamerican.com/beautiful-minds/openness-to-experience-and-creative-achievement/

Kim, K. H. (2010). The creativity crisis in the United States. In *Online Encyclopedia Britannica* (p. 2).

Kolovelonis, A., Goudas, M., & Dermitzaki, I. (2011). The effect of different goals and self-recording on self-regulation of learning a motor skill in a physical education setting. *Learning and instruction, 21*(3), 355–364.

Krueger, J. (2016). *Maslow on creativity*. Retrieved from psychologytoday.com/blog/one-among-many/201309/maslow-creativity

Kurzweil, R. (2006). *The singularity is near*. New York, NY: Viking.

Kurzweil, R. (2012). *How to create a mind: The secret of human thought revealed*. New York, NY: Penguin.

Labuhn, A. S., Zimmerman, B. J., & Hasselhorn, M. (2010). Enhancing students' self-regulation and mathematics performance: The influence of feedback and self-evaluative standards. *Metacognition and learning, 5*(2), 173–194.

Lawrie, G. (2017). *How our school is using virtual reality to prepare pupils for a future dominated by technology*. Retrieved from telegraph.co.uk/education/2017/01/23/school-using-virtual-reality-prepare-pupils-future-dominated/

Levitt, S., & others. (2013). *The behavioralist goes to school: Leveraging behavioral economics to improve educational performance*. Chicago, IL: University of Chicago Press.

Manocha, R. (2010). Meditation, mindfulness and mind-emptiness. *Science Alert*. Retrieved from cambridge.org

Maslow, A. H. (1998). *Toward a psychology of being*, 3/e. New York: John Wiley & Sons, Inc.

Mass. ESSE. (2017). *Guidelines on implementing social and emotional learning (SEL) curricula: K-12*. Boston, MA: Statehouse.

Masten, A. S. (2014). Global perspectives on resilience in children and youth. *Child Development, 85*(1): 6–20. doi:10.1111/cdev.12205

Meador, D. (2017, May). *Problems for teachers that limit their overall effectiveness*. Retrieved from thoughtco.com/derrick-meador-3194224

Meador, T. (2018). *Media literacy now*.

Merrell, K. & Gueldner, B. (2010). *Social and emotional learning in the classroom: Promoting mental health and academic success*. New York: Guilford Press.

National School Reform Faculty. (2014). *Text rendering experience*. Harmony Education Center. Retrieved from nsrfharmony.org/.

NCTM. (2016). *Beginning to problem solve with "I notice, I wonder."* Retrieved from http://mathforum.org/pubs/notice_wonder_intro.pdf

Nhat Hanh, T. (2008). Work: How to find joy and meaning in each hour of the day. New York, NY: Penguin.

Oxford University Summer School. (2018). *20 argumentative essay topics for middle school*. It's Time to Learn More About Essay Writing. Retrieved from oxforduniversitysummerschool.com

Paulos, J. (2016, July). *Do sat scores really predict success?* Retrieved from http://abcnews.go.com/technology/whoscounting/story?id=98373

Payton, J., & others. (2015). *The positive impact of social and emotional learning for kindergarten to eighth-grade student: Findings from three scientific reviews*. Retrieved from CASEL.org.

Pekel, E., Roehlkepartain, C., & Syvertsen, A. (2018, April 11). *In support of self-report surveys*. Retrieved from measuringsel.casel.org/defense-self-report-surveys/

Ribas, W., Brady, D., & Hardin, J. (2017). *Social-emotional learning in the classroom: A practical guide for integrating all SEL skills into instruction and classroom management*. Norwood, MA: Ribas Pub.

Rifkin, J. (2009). *The empathic civilization*. New York, NY: Penguin.

Ripple, R., & Dacey, J. (1967). Communication, education, and creativity. *Contemporary Educational Psychology*, 219–231.

Roth, M. (2010, January 3). *Beyond critical thinking*. Retrieved from https://www.chronicle.com/article/Beyond-Critical-Thinking/63288

Ryan, J. (2012). *Struggle for inclusion*. Charlotte, NC: Information Age Publishing.

Schank, R., & Cleary, C. (1995). *Making machines creative*. Cambridge, MA: MIT University Press.

Schunk, D., & Zimmerman, B. (2007). Influencing children's self-efficacy and self-regulation of reading and writing through modeling. *Reading & Writing Quarterly, 23*(1), 7–25.

Scientific American. (2018). *How to cultivate your creativity*. Retrieved from scientificamerican.com/article/how-to-cultivate-your-creativity-book-excerpt/

Scriven, M., & Paul, R. (1987). *Critical thinking definitions*. Paper read at the 8th Annual International Conference on Critical Thinking and Education Reform.

Seitel, M. (2009). Mindfulness in a school community. In I. McHenry & R. Brady (Eds.), *Tuning in: Mindfulness in teaching & learning*. Philadelphia, PA: Friends Council on Education.

Selman, R. (1981). The child as a friendship philosopher. In S. R. Asher & J. M. Gottman (Eds.), *The development of children's friendships* (pp. 242–272). Cambridge, UK: Cambridge University Press.

Selman, R. (2003). *The promotion of social awareness*. New York, NY: Russell Sage Foundation.

Selye, H. (1976). *The stress of life* (rev. edn.). New York: McGraw-Hill.

Shapiro, D., et al. (1993). A psychological "sense-of-control" profile of patients with anorexia nervosa and bulimia nervosa. *Psychological Reports: 73*, 531–541.

Shirley, A. (2016, p. 1). *Five charts that explain the future of education*. Retrieved from weforum.org/agenda/2016/05/5-charts-that-explain-the-future-of-education/

Sipos, D. (2014). *Untangled*. Retrieved from beatport.com/track/untangled-feat-dana-sipos-extended-mix/9206815

6Seconds. (2017). *Learn about EQ*. 6Seconds.org

Slavin, R. (2013). *Why use cooperative learning?* Starting Point: Teaching Entry Level Geoscience. Retrieved from https://serc.carleton.edu/introgeo/cooperative/whyuse.html

Spencer, S., NCTM. (2017). *I notice, I wonder.* Retrieved from mathforum.org/pubs/notice_wonder_intro.pdf

Sternberg, R., & Lubart, T. (1995). *Defying the crowd.* New York: Free Press.

Stevens, T. (2015). *The case for being a generous leader: Are you a generous leader or a selfish one?* http://www.fastcompany.com/3043572/

Talloires Symposium. (2017). *Civics commitment.* Retrieved from fletcher.tufts.edu/Alumni/Events/Talloires-2016/Talloires

Taylor, R., & others. (2017, July). *The Taylor review.* Retrieved from assets.publishing.service.gov.uk/government/uploads/system/uploads/attachment_data/file/627671/good-work-taylor-review-modern-working-practices-rg.pdf

Torrance, E. (2000). *Voyages of discovering creativity.* New York: Praeger.

Tsabary, S. (2010). *The conscious parent: Transforming ourselves, empowering our children.* Vancouver, Canada: Namaste Publishing.

UUA. (2018). *Our whole lives: Lifespan sexuality education.* Retrieved from uua.org/re/owl

van Noorden, T., & others. (2016). Bullying involvement and empathy: child and target characteristics. *Social Development, 26*(2): 248–262.

Walsh, D. C., (2006). *Trustworthy Leadership.* Fetzer Institute.

WebMD. (2017). *5 teen behavior problems: A troubleshooting guide.* Retrieved from webmd.com/parenting/teen-abuse-cough-medicine-9/behavior-problems

Weinbaum, S. (1935). *Pygmalian's glasses.* [EBook #22893] *56,* 231–237.

Weinberger, M. (2017, April 2). The smartphone is eventually going to die, and then things are going to get really crazy. *Business Insider.* Retrieved from business insider.in/the-smartphone-is-eventually-going-to-die-and-then-things-are-going-to-get-really-crazy/articleshow/57977438.cms

Weissberg, R. (2016). *Consensus statement to the U.S. D.O.E.* Chicago, IL: CASEL (Collaborative for Academic, Social and Emotional Learning).

Weissberg, R. (2017). *Why social and emotional learning is essential for students.* Retrieved from edutopia.org/blog/why

Weng, H. Y., Fox, A. S., Shackman, A. J., Stodola, D. E., Caldwell, J. Z. K., Olson, M. C., Rogers, G. M., & Davidson, R. J. (2013). Compassion training alters altruism and the neural responses to suffering. *Psychological Science, 24,* 1171–1180.

Wikipedia. (2018). *Dunning–Kruger effect.* Retrieved from en.wikipedia.org/wiki/Dunning—Kruger_effect

Zakrzewski, F. (2015). *Social-emotional learning: Why now?* Retrieved from huffingtonpost.com/vicki-zakrzewski-phd/social-emotional-learning-why-now_b_6466918.html

Zhao, Y. (2014). *Who's afraid of the big bad dragon: Why China has the best (and worst) education system in the world.* San Francisco, CA: Jossey-Bass/Wiley.

Zimmerman, B. J. (2000). Attaining self-regulation: a social cognitive perspective. In M. Boekaerts, P. R. Pintrich, & M. Zeidner, (Eds.), *Handbook of self-regulation.* San Diego: CA: Academic Press.

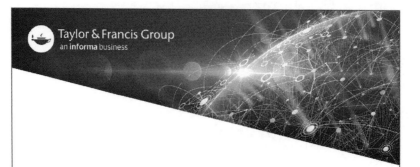

Made in the USA
Middletown, DE
23 July 2021